Teacher Education in England and Wales

Geoffrey Partington
Flinders University
South Australia

Published by the IEA Education and Training Unit
1999

First published in September 1999 by
The Institute of Economic Affairs
2 Lord North Street
Westminster
London SW1P 3LB

© IEA 1999

IEA Studies in Education No. 8
All rights reserved

ISBN 0 255 36476 8

Many IEA publications are translated into languages other than English or are reprinted. Permission to translate or to reprint should be sought from the General Director at the address above.

Printed in Great Britain by
Hartington Fine Arts Limited, Lancing, West Sussex
Set in Century Schoolbook and Bookman Old Style

Contents

	Foreword	5
	The Author	8
	Acknowledgements	9
	An Outline	10
	A personal note	13
	The perspective of the argument	16
1.	**The Historical Background**	19
	The teacher-missionaries	19
	The cultivated teacher	23
	The teacher as transformer of society	31
	The child-centred teacher	36
2.	**Ideological Capture by the New Left**	40
	The New Left and civic virtue	40
	The New Left and liberal knowledge	42
	The New Left and child-centred education	45
	The New Left and revolutionary defeatism	50
	The situation in 1979	59
3.	**The Conservative Reforms**	69
	New Right critiques	79
	Responses within ITT to Conservative reforms	83
4.	**My 1997 Interviews**	94
	Attitudes to OFSTED and the TTA	94
	Partnerships between HEIs and schools	102
	Educational theory	109
5.	**SCITT**	113

6.	**Ideological Capture**	118
	Race and gender	118
	Some other ITT courses	124
	Teacher educators and research	132
7.	**Which Way Ahead?**	140
	The case for more prescription	140
	The case for more freedom	142
	The limits of contestability	146
	The positive role of ITT	148
	Conclusion	157
Appendix A	**Some Reading Lists**	159
	University of Manchester	159
	Manchester Metropolitan University	160
	University of Warwick Institute of Education	161
Glossary		162

Foreword

Dr Partington's study of teacher education in England and Wales is greatly to be welcomed. If, as Partington says education is an essentially contested concept, teacher training must be even more so, as it is there that the contest will be at its most pointed.

As a member of the Council for the Accreditation of Teacher Education from 1990 to 1994, and then of the Teacher Training Agency from 1994 to 1997, I can confirm that there was and continues to be a fierce contest over teacher training. Those involved in teacher education bitterly resent any criticism of their practices from those they perceive to be outsiders, whether they are elected governments, academics from disciplines other than education, employers, parents or just concerned members of the public.

During the period in which I was involved in teacher training the government was indeed determined to bring about radical changes in teacher training, though its intentions were routinely subverted by bureaucrats who had agendas of their own and traduced by the providers of teacher training. Some of this story appears in Dr Partington's book. Precisely because of the bitterness and misinformation rife in the period in question, Partington's study is timely. It is informed and fair minded, not unsympathetic to teacher trainers or to the concept of teacher education, yet not uncritical either. Part of its value derives from the fact that it is written by someone from the other side of the world, who is not a party to the struggles or controversies as they have developed in this country, but who knows enough about the area to comment on it perceptively.

In attempting to change the ethos of teacher training, the government was not indulging in luddism or iconoclasm for their own sakes. It was responding to what it saw, rightly in my view, to be a desperate crisis in state education in Britain. Of course, to those who failed to notice that there was a crisis, policies designed to remove the monopoly of teacher supply from higher education departments of education could well appear purely destructive. But to the critics of state education and its standards, the root cause of the problem lay precisely in those departments, in their refusal to admit that there was a problem other than 'under-funding', and in the dogmas about education which ruled within them, which blinded them to what was perfectly obvious to everyone else who considered the matter. The point is that no one could become a teacher in a state school in this country who was not certified by a system in which certain doctrines antithetical to educational achievement were deeply embedded. Again Partington makes valuable points about the nature of those dogmas, and also about the pernicious mixture of complacency and defensiveness which obtains within the world of teacher training.

Education is, as has been said, an essentially contested area. The trouble with state education in Britain at the end of the twentieth century is that for too long only one view has been heard. There has been no contest, none of the healthy competition of ideas – and practices – which Partington would like to see. 'Theory' in educational circles has not been an arena for intellectual engagement. Rather it has been a pretext for the dreary rehearsal of second-rate ideologies by academics unready for intellectual opposition, and for the refusal to qualify students who did not pay at least lip-service to them. Again Partington provides examples.

What, then, is to be done? How does one break up a monolith, particularly one funded by the state and dominated by self-serving ideas and nostrums? While Partington is certainly aware of the problem, and will for that reason incur hostility and opprobrium, I feel he could have been more radical. Without denying the role of theory – proper theory – in teacher training he could have said more about the desirability of basing teacher training in the best schools, schools which are not dominated by child-centred and skills-based approaches. He is right to observe that there is no point in basing teacher training in poor schools or in schools wedded to methods known to be questionable, but maybe our best hope in the short term is to seek out excellent schools, and to make them educational analogues of teaching hospitals.

But, it will be said, surely these schools must be validated, certified and given governmental seals of approval. And, so by means of whatever agency the government sets up, the old cycle of mediocrity and dogma inherent in any state-centralised system re-emerges. This, of course, is the paradox of trying at the same time to free up and control a system, to which Partington alludes. All I can say, from my experience of the Teacher Training Agency, is that it does not work. There is an inevitable regression to bureaucratically enforced mediocrity as every lobby group and provider interest clambers aboard the already creaking and obsolescent omnibus, welcomed in by the civil servants supposedly driving it. To continue the analogy, would it not be better from the point of view of the general public to give them access to a range of private vehicles which they could choose and drive themselves, as they saw fit?

In other words, would it not be better, given that education is an essentially contested area, to allow parents and others the freedom to select the schools and educational methods of their choice? This would, of course, have profound effects on teacher training, for the schools would then be free to choose and train their teachers as they saw fit, and not as centralists in government departments saw fit. (Partington rightly underlines the undesirability of large scale prescription by central government in this area.) The prospects for liberalising reforms under the present government are unfortunately virtually nil, if we are to go by its attacks on educational freedoms in its recent centralising legislation. But then the signs are hardly more auspicious in Mr Hague's 'Conservative' party, which suggests to me that we just do not have politicians at the moment with the vision or drive to do anything sufficiently radical about education in general or about teacher training in particular.

ANTHONY O'HEAR
University of Bradford

The Author

Geoffrey Partington was educated in Middleton, Lancashire, at Boarshaw Primary School and Queen Elizabeth's Grammar School and subsequently at the Universities of Bristol and London. He received an honours degree in history and a master's degree in education from Bristol University, an honours degree in sociology, a PGCE and the Academic Diploma in Education from London University, and a PhD from the University of Adelaide.

After National Service in the Royal Air Force, Partington taught history for twelve years in Glendale Grammar School, Wood Green, and then Twyford Comprehensive School, Acton. Subsequently he was a senior lecturer in history at Doncaster College of Education and in education at Coventry College of Education. He became headmaster of Bungay Modern School in Suffolk and an Education Officer in the London Borough of Waltham Forest. After emigrating to Australia in 1976 he taught at Flinders University of South Australia, where he is still a Visiting Scholar. After retirement from teaching at Flinders University he taught for two years at the University of the South Pacific in Suva, Fiji.

Partington's books include *Women Teachers in the Twentieth Century* (1976) and *The Idea of an Historical Education* (1980), both published by the National Foundation of Education Publishing Company, Windsor, *The Australian Nation: Its British and Irish Roots* (1994), published by Australian Scholarly Publishing, Melbourne (American Edition, 1997, by Transaction Publishers, New Brunswick), *Hasluck versus Coombs: White Politics and Australia's Aborigines* (1996), published by Quaker Hill Press, Sydney, and *Teacher Education and Training in New Zealand* (1997), published by The Education Forum, Wellington.

Acknowledgements

I am grateful to the teacher educators who gave their time for my 1997 interviews. I am also grateful to the reviewers appointed by the Institute of Economic Affairs who provided valuable advice on the manuscript I submitted to it for possible publication. Any virtues in my analysis are largely due to that advice, but the errors which remain are entirely my own. I hope that readers will show me some indulgence: since I have lived for nearly a quarter of a century in distant Australia it is very likely that I have failed to take account of some important changes in the professional preparation of teachers in Britain during those years. Yet the perspective of an interested outsider who was once an active participant may add something to the insights of those far closer to the ground than I have been in recent years.

An Outline

After a personal note I argue that education is an essentially contestable activity and base the case for educational choice upon this fundamental idea. Chapter 1 looks at ways in which all five clusters of educational thought I identify contributed to teacher education during the nineteenth and twentieth centuries. Initial Teacher Training (ITT) for elementary teachers was for a long time mainly of an instrumentalist character, but one with strong moral undertones, with the emerging teachers seen as social missionaries to the masses, whereas ITT for secondary (grammar school) teachers was of a much more liberal character. Strong 'Old Left' reconstructionist sentiments were held by many teachers and those who trained them, and the twentieth century saw a rapid expansion in the influence of child-centred ideas, especially in the colleges. Many colleges were religious in origins, and Roman Catholic schools until recently relied substantially on religious orders for their teachers, but similarities between the sense of mission of the secularist social missionary teacher and the committed transcendentalist were then more important than differences between them. The great expansion in teacher education in the 1950s and 1960s, the decades of hope, is then considered.

During the 1960s, it is argued in Chapter 2, the main educational programme of the 'Old Left' was implemented by the Labour Party and largely accepted by the Conservative Party. Its effects soon seemed pathetically inadequate to many of its most ardent advocates, with the result that a 'New Left' emerged which combined demands for increasingly radical educational changes with ever-deepening doubts that these could achieve significant effects this side of the revolution, an event no more desired by most New Left educationists than anyone else. Many on the New Left came to loathe the way in which the Old Left, and most other teacher educators, had until recently sought to 'gentle the masses'. Another object of New Left distaste was any form of testing which might reveal whether or not their own policies were succeeding. A sceptical 'new sociology of knowledge' rejecting distinctions between knowledge and belief became increasingly fashionable in ITT. The most negative elements from reconstructionist and child-centred convictions entered into temporary alliance. It was the educational hour of Risinghill and William Tyndale.

Chapter 3 examines the policies for teacher education of the Thatcher and Major governments, and suggests there was always potential instability in their attempt to combine 'bottom-up' and 'top-down' reform. Genuine concern, inherited and extended by Tony Blair and David Blunkett, at the destructive effects of many New Left policies led the Conservatives to strengthen the central educational powers of the state, including the Teacher Training Agency (TTA), the Office for Standards in Education (OFSTED) and a National Curriculum for Initial Teacher Training. These efforts to improve standards outweighed in importance significant relaxations in routes into teaching, leading ultimately to the school-centred initiatives. Thinkers grouped by their enemies into a largely undifferentiated 'New Right' were united in their dislike of New Left excesses in ITT, but some wanted to mend educational theory and ITT as a whole, whereas others despaired of mending ITT which, short of ending entirely, they sought to relocate as much as possible in the schools. The growing gap between 'menders' and 'enders' was clearly revealed by the rupture between Brian Cox and some of his closest allies during his Black Paper days. Teacher education bodies such as the Universities Council for the Education of Teachers (UCET) bitterly opposed every change the Conservatives made. As time moved on, the pre-1979 years seemed ever more idyllic to official spokespersons for the education industry.

Chapter 4 consists in large part of reportage and analysis of my 1997 interviews with 36 teacher educators. The issues particularly explored were their attitudes towards OFSTED and the TTA, towards the new system of partnerships between Higher Educational Institutions (HEIs) and schools, towards School-Centred Initial Teacher Training (SCITT), although few of my informants had direct experience of SCITT, and towards the place of educational theory within ITT and of educational research in HEIs. My overall impression was that most of my informants shared much of the hostility towards OFSTED and the TTA expressed in their names by their professional organisations, but that almost all of them believed that their own institution had better relationships with the schools in 1997 than when the Conservative reforms began and that their own ITT programmes were more efficient and relevant to the needs of schools and beginning teachers than in the past.

Chapter 5 shows that rampant ideological bias continued in 1997 to distort some compulsory courses in ITT which purport to combat racism and sexism. There is every reason to fear that these are areas in which 'New Left' teacher educators concentrated some of their forces as the amount of educational theory in ITT shrank. A few courses which I encountered outside anti-racism and anti-sexism were also indoctrinative in character, but these may not be representative. However, there are good grounds for fearing that some methods courses, especially in science teaching, in which a radical form of constructivism is currently dominant, and in teaching how to teach reading, fail to provide student teachers with a balanced introduction to pedagogical problems.

Chapter 6 considers the main current options in ITT for liberal-conservatives. It acknowledges that the abuses which became so extensive during the 1970s seemed to require stern top-down reforms and that the National Curriculum for ITT, as implemented by the TTA, has significantly raised standards of professional preparation for beginning teachers. It concedes that bottom-up reforms, including making SCITT an alternative to HEI-based ITT courses as well as opening up other new routes into teaching, may well have been insufficient to raise standards of practical efficiency into ITT at an acceptable pace. However, the path of greater freedom of choice is preferred to that of detailed prescription, as is only to be expected given that I begin from the standpoint of education as an essentially contestable activity. I urge that, despite the mischief wrought by many educationists, the proper answer to bad educational theory is good educational theory, not an attempt to make teaching a non-theoretical amalgam of practical skills. I argue that it would be better if the National Curriculum for ITT were exemplary rather than mandatory, with HEIs and SCITT schools allowed to offer alternative courses but the responsibility to demonstrate that these meet the key objectives of the National Curriculum falling on the providers and on employers of beginning teachers.

A personal note

Since I have lived in Australia since 1976, some explanation ought to be given for my offering an assessment of teacher education in Britain. I was a 'scholarship' child from a primary school on a council estate in a Lancashire mill town. The school opened in 1937, but it was only in 1941 that I became one of its first pupils to 'pass the 11+' and go on to grammar school. I was the first child in my family to go to a university and my place at Bristol University was secured through a four-year bursary, which included a Post-Graduate Certificate of Education year after three years of undergraduate study for an honours degree. Had it not been for the bursary, I would have gone directly into national service and might not have entered a university subsequently. After national service I enrolled in London University Institute of Education in 1953 for a PGCE year.

During my 23 years in England as an educator I had two spells in colleges of education, as a senior lecturer in history at Doncaster College of Education and a senior lecturer in education at Coventry College of Education, now part of the University of Warwick. As a teacher in Glendale Grammar School, Wood Green, and Twyford Comprehensive School, Acton, my classes were regularly used for teaching practices by London University Institute of Education, where for some years, as a young teacher, I pursued further academic study, gaining its Academic Diploma of Education with distinction in 1957. I started on a thesis on Richard Burdon Haldane as an educational thinker, but did not complete it, mainly through excessive involvement in the affairs of the National Union of Teachers, the Campaign for Nuclear Disarmament and the Communist Party. Both in the NUT and the Communist Party I served on committees concerned with educational policies, and was often assigned responsibility for drafting statements on reports, such as Robbins and Plowden, which dealt *inter alia* with teacher education. When I was headmaster of Bungay Modern School, Suffolk, I was invited to lecture in Keswick Hall College, Norwich, as well as hosting student teachers. As an Education Officer in the London Borough of Waltham Forest, my last post before emigrating to Australia, I renewed contact with London University Institute of Education by representing the Essex Outer London Education Authorities on its In-service Planning Committee.

A slow learner, I did not break with the Communist Party until 1968, when Soviet troops invaded Czechoslovakia. I joined the Labour Party in 1972 and was still a member when I emigrated to Australia in 1976. I am now not a socialist of any school. I had deep misgivings about many aspects of Marxism and other varieties of socialism, as well as about the policies of governments which claimed to embody such ideas, long before 1968, but the investment of many years of moral and intellectual capital since 1948, when I first joined the Bristol University Student Branch of the Communist Party, and close friendships with many old comrades, made departure even more difficult than sticking it out. Most, perhaps all, of my own changes in political sentiment may be largely irrelevant to whether analyses I now offer of teacher education are worthy of consideration, but it may be helpful to readers to know what continuities and discontinuities there have been in my thinking on educational questions.

It is sometimes asked why communists were often elected to important offices in teacher unions by members who would not have dreamed of voting for them in national or local political elections. Part of the explanation lay in the zeal and persistence of party comrades in organisations which most members join mainly for professional protection should anything go wrong in the classroom and have very limited interest in attending meetings. At least equally important, however, were the educational values which large numbers of left-leaning teachers shared with communists, who were often the most active and capable exponents of those values. Educational beliefs held in common by both Marxists and non-Marxists within the 'Old Left' were far more considerable than those in which they significantly differed. The central grounds of agreement were three:

- that, despite some inevitable contestability, it was both possible and necessary to identify types of knowledge and understanding needed for full development as individuals and citizens;
- that such knowledge and understanding should be extended to the masses and not confined to privileged groups in society;
- that such knowledge and understanding was largely of a universal character and needed by males and females alike

and by all peoples, although time and place necessarily influenced choices of examples to illustrate general truths.

These have remained my own basic convictions, whether as communist, Labour Party member and 'neo-conservative' or whatever descriptor may now best apply to me. Although I came to reject some of the means I once thought would best promote the extension of liberal knowledge, in basic aims I remain much more like the 'Old Left' than do many of the post-1960s 'New Left'.

As a teacher educator in an Australian university since 1976, I have, of course, spent more time on the study of Australian education than that elsewhere. I have also spent considerable time in studying teacher education and school systems in New Zealand and in Fiji and the South Pacific. I also retained my interests in education in general, especially teacher education, in the United Kingdom, and was keen to follow up my 1996 survey of teacher education in New Zealand[1] with something comparable, if less comprehensive, in England and Wales.

During the years of the Thatcher and Major governments, I became increasingly struck as I read the British educational press by an apparent inconsistency between allegations that the changes introduced into teacher education by the Conservatives were highly destructive in their effects and claims by virtually every HEI that its own standards of efficiency and relationships with schools in respect of teaching practice had improved significantly since 1979 and were continuing to improve. In order to clarify this apparent contradiction, in 1997 I asked a number of teacher educators to meet me and to inform me about changes in their own institutions and their own views on the Conservative reforms as a whole. The original names were chosen on the basis of articles published in the leading relevant refereed professional journals; there was no ideological element in the selection. In some cases the person I hoped to interview was not available, but in others the targeted individuals not only made themselves available but suggested to me colleagues who were also in a good position to provide me with relevant information. The teacher educators I finally met were

---

1 See Partington, G. (1997). *Teacher Education and Training in New Zealand*. Wellington: Education Forum.

Terry Martin of the University of Southampton, David Lambert of the London University Institute of Education, Jim Campbell of Warwick University, Len Barton and Peter Gilroy of Sheffield University, James Tooley of Manchester University, David Carr of the Heriot-Watt University, Edinburgh, Rod Bramald, Frank Hardman, David Leat and Tony Edwards of the University of Newcastle upon Tyne, Jerry Norton of the University of Sunderland, John Furlong of Bristol University, Roger Trend of the University of Exeter and Denis Hayes of the University of Plymouth.

Most interviews were taped and, whenever there was ambiguity in my tapes and notes, I submitted my version for correction and accepted the revised account. My interviews were confined to staff in teacher education institutions, since it was impossible for me to meet a representative range of school-based mentors and other interested parties. Although none of the people interviewed claimed to represent the official views of their institutions, I have no reason now, any more than when I set off on the interviews, to consider that they were unrepresentative of their colleagues as a whole. In any case, I claim no more for these interviews than that they reflect the considered views of some experienced teacher educators. On all my visits I was provided with a wide range of course outlines and other relevant publications.

The perspective of the argument

I start from the perspective that education is an essentially contestable activity, in Gallie's sense that thoughtful people may know all the relevant facts and yet hold conflicting priorities and values.[2] Empirical evidence is rarely in itself sufficient to persuade adherents to any one cluster to abandon it for another, although relevant evidence may well lead to changes in means adopted to secure aims and purposes. Education in this respect is similar to politics: very different values and priorities are held by people of comparable intelligence and experience and the failure of particular policies is seldom sufficient to lead to the abandonment of values and priorities.

---

2 See Gallie, W. H. (1968). *Philosophy and Historical Understanding.* Schocken Books, New York, pp. 161 ff.

Educational theories may be divided into five clusters, each with a different priority:

- *transcendental education*: what is thought to be of greatest value to God's purposes
- *instrumental education*: what is thought to be of greatest value to society broadly as it is or to the individual purposes of each person
- *liberal education*: what is thought to be of greatest value to the development of the mind through the acquisition of the most significant types of knowledge
- *reconstructionist education*: what is thought to be of greatest value in transforming society as it is to one of a radically different character
- *child-centred education*: what is thought to be of greatest value or interest to the child.

Within each cluster, too, there are, of course, many choices of an essentially contestable character. Instrumentalists disagree what is of greatest value to a society at any given moment. Argument about just what constitutes the different society which ought to be created and how education might best accelerate the process is often sharp among reconstructionists. Each distinctive religion, while urging the priority of transcendental over world values, has a very different set of beliefs about the nature of God and the created world. Some child-centred educators concentrate on trying to detect and satisfy the educational needs of each individual child, but others on those of children in general. Liberal educators, from Plato and Aristotle onwards, have disagreed about which knowledge is of most worth to the development of mind or of the understanding. However, the importance of disputes within the clusters identified does not weaken the significance of contestation between them.

A particular educational practice, idea or theory is not necessarily drawn entirely from a single cluster but, although ideas arising from two or more clusters may be in harmony for a time, there inevitably arise 'moments of truth' in which choices must be made between values which prove to be incompatible. For example, 'New Left' educational ideas which became influential during the 1960s in teacher education in several liberal-democratic societies included significant elements from both child-centred and reconstructionist clusters, but a moment of truth arrived for many feminist teachers. They found that they had to choose between encouraging children to follow their own interests, as child-centred ideas seemed to require, with the consequence that 'traditionally gender-related' interests were replicated, and opposing children's preferences so that girls and boys would ultimately become more like each other in their interests and curriculum choices, as current reconstructionism required.

Essential contestability is one of the main justifications for choice in education in general, as well as for opening up a variety of routes into teaching, but contestability should not be confused with permissiveness. Some conditions must be fulfilled before an educational theory can be regarded as formally coherent and enter into serious educational contestation. Some conditions are internal: a coherent theory must explain which educational needs it purports to meet, to what authority it appeals for its claims, and on what grounds it considers knowledge to be legitimated. A coherent theory must possess standards by which proponents and opponents alike can make informed judgements about the extent to which its aims and objectives are being achieved. Other conditions relate to minimum requirements which, in open societies, the state should insist be satisfied before it gives legal status, let alone financial support, to educational institutions. Some of these requirements are prescriptive, such as that schools should ensure that their students are enabled to acquire literacy, numeracy and various skills and forms of substantive knowledge. Other requirements are proscriptive, such as that schools should not incite their students to break the law of the land or to infringe the rights of other members of civil society. However, the key point here is that there are coherent and consistent forms of each of the five clusters of educational ideas which can legitimately be held by the most thoughtful and experienced among us. So long as they are willing to submit their operations and results to public scrutiny, both at parental and governmental level, and do not seek to infringe the freedoms of others, adherents of coherent versions of each cluster should be entitled to open schools and to provide distinctive types of teacher education.

1 | The Historical Background

There are four main types of teacher which teacher education since 1945 has tried to produce. These relate to four of the five clusters of educational theories identified above: instrumental, liberal, reconstructionist and child-centred. Separate attention to transcendentalist beliefs is not given here. This is because in their operational requirements, as distinct from their ultimate grounds for these, transcendentalist educators were little different from the secularist 'teacher-missionaries'. I have divided instrumentalist teachers into two groups: the first, who emphasise broad moral and civic needs of society, I include with the 'teacher-missionaries'; and the second, whose first concern is to produce 'effective' teachers and to meet employment and vocational needs, I consider in the context of the Conservative reforms of the 1980s.

The teacher-missionaries

The training colleges had their origins in the 'normal colleges' founded in the 1830s by reformers such as Sir James Kay-Shuttleworth. Most of their students for most of the nineteenth century were former elementary school pupils who became pupil-teachers at the age of thirteen or fourteen, although for many years most pupil-teachers never succeeded in getting to college and remained uncertificated or received certification on the basis of on-the-job ability, as judged by national inspectors. Arthur Balfour noted, when introducing what became the 1902 Education Act, that 55 per cent of the elementary teaching force had never set foot in a training college. The 1902 Act established that in future elementary teachers should themselves receive a secondary, not an elementary, education, and it enabled the new Local Education Authorities (LEAs) to establish municipal training colleges, which were in time to outnumber the voluntary foundations of the churches. The pupil-teachers who had attended a college received a handsome tribute from a Board of Education report in 1924:

> For more than half a century many of the brighter children passed into the profession by way of pupil-teachership, and supplied the training colleges with a succession of hard-working students of whom, whatever their academic attainments, it might be certainly said that they knew how to teach.[3]

William Taylor suggested that most of the training colleges offered 'a diluted form of gracious living engaged in by a largely spinster staff, in an impressive if educationally unsuitable and draughty building at the end of a mile-long drive, ten miles from the nearest town'.[4] However, the students were heirs to a long tradition of tough-mindedness and were rarely ignorant of the evils and woes of the world. There was very little of child-centredness in the old elementary tradition. Recalling his own elementary schooldays, Lionel Elvin wrote

> Curriculum and methods were by our standards very rigid and old-fashioned. We really did the cotton towns of Lancashire, and the capes and rivers of England, and we recited our multiplication tables, and we had spelling drill. And we recited Kingsley's 'Cool and Clear', Longfellow's 'Village Blacksmith' and Wordsworth's 'Daffodils'; and of course the 'Magnificat'.[5]

Most of the early colleges were founded by churches and affiliated religious organisations, so that 'teacher-missionaries', a term first used by Jean Floud, is appropriate to the type of teacher they sought to shape.[6] As late as 1968 the 166 colleges of education in England and Wales included twenty-seven Anglican

---

3 Board of Education: Cmd. 2409 (1925). *Report of the Departmental Committee on the Training of Teachers in Public Elementary Schools.* London: HMSO, p. 12.
4 Taylor, W. (1969). *Society and the Education of Teachers.* London: Faber & Faber, p. 205.
5 Elvin, H. L. (1971). 'Colleges of Education: Their Achievements and Prospects' in F. H. Hilliard (ed). *Teaching the Teachers: Trends in Teacher Education.* London: George Allen and Unwin, p. 25. Professor Hilliard of Birmingham University evidently did not trust a college lecturer to write this chapter in his book.
6 Floud, J. E. (1962). 'Teaching in the Affluent Society' in *British Journal of Sociology,* XIII (4).

foundations, seventeen Roman Catholic, and nine Methodist and nonconformist Protestant. However, many of the 113 purely secular colleges had been infused in the past with what Robert Bellah termed 'civil religion', the ethos of the early twentieth-century American schoolhouse as well as the English elementary school, and were committed to a moral order derived from traditional Judeo-Christian teaching.[7] Most of the elementary school teachers saw themselves as having a civilising role, as well as imparting the '3 Rs' with maximum efficiency, and the teaching certificate was usually a reliable guarantee of both moral respectability and vocational competence. The aim of 'gentling the masses', or 'spreading sweetness and light', was dear to many trade unionists and socialists, as well as the Christian churches. By the 1930s this concept had some detractors, such as the American sociologist Willard Waller, who sneered at those who sought to make the school into a 'museum of virtue', promulgating values rarely practised in the outside world.[8] Nonetheless, the 'civic religion' retained much of its power until the 1960s, when sneers at 'social control' and 'imposing middle-class values' became common in teacher education. Lionel Elvin acknowledged that the old elementary teachers 'shared in the broad social movement which increasingly enabled the working people of England to move from hierarchal subordination to something like democratic citizenship', and regretted in 1971, 'We are so afraid of being implicated in the narrow orthodoxies of the past that we will not admit that we do want children to grow up into good men and women.'[9]

In the 1950s the training colleges still conceived of themselves as moral communities. Great concern was taken with the character of the student-teachers, both in selection and in progress through college. Student-teachers were closely watched, in groups of a dozen or so, by education tutors who had previously enjoyed success as classroom teachers or head teachers with the relevant age range of children and whose qualifications for appointment normally included that they were morally exemplary. A later generation of teacher educators with more

---

7 See Bellah, R. N. (1975). *The Broken Contract: American Civil Religion in a Time of Trial*. New York: Seabury Press.
8 Waller, W. (1932). *The Sociology of Teaching*. New York: John Wiley.
9 Elvin, 1971, p. 22–3.

scholarly aspirations was inclined to smile when recalling the age of the 'mother hens', but the influence of the latter was usually powerful, partly because there was very limited specialisation. Each college had one or more lecturers with special interests in reading, number, science, music and so on, and there were usually courses in educational ideas given by a lecturer, sometimes the college principal, with wider than usual theoretical interests, but specialist 'disciplines of education' were unknown, apart from a few colleges which offered separate courses in educational psychology. Sully's *Teachers Handbook of Psychology* went into five editions between 1886 and 1909. Psychology courses during the twentieth century were increasingly influenced by two very different sets of ideas: concepts of intelligence advanced by Thorndyke, Terman and Spearman; and the developmental approach of Piaget.[10]

Even this amount of specialisation did not meet with universal approval. In 1943 the McNair Committee expressed the fear that 'in some university training departments, and perhaps in some training colleges, specialist lecturers in psychology, in particular, exact too large a proportion of the time available and expect too much of their students'.[11] The McNair Report anticipated Kenneth Clarke by nearly half a century by recommending that some of the practical work in ITT should take place in schools under the supervision of head teachers and senior staff rather than in the colleges, as did T. H. B. Hollins of Leeds University in 1971.[12] It is thus false to claim that the ideas later embodied in SCITT had never been aired since the days of the pupil-teachers. 'Main subjects' were offered in the 1950s, but little emphasis was placed on them. It was usually assumed that the education tutors were sufficiently well informed to guide students through most of the primary curriculum to a 'main subject' level. It would be unfair to depict the 1950s training colleges as anti-intellectual, but most of their staffs considered the formation of character to be of pre-eminent importance.

---

10 See Tibble, J. W. (1963). 'Psychological Theories and Teacher Training' in G. Z. F. Bereday and J. A. Lauwerys (eds). *The Education and Training of Teachers*. London: Evans Brothers.
11 McNair Committee (1943). *Teachers and Youth Leaders*. London: HMSO, p. 68.
12 Hollins, T. H. B. (1971). 'Desirable Changes in the Structure of Courses' in F. H. Hilliard (ed). *Teaching the Teachers: Trends in Teacher Education*. London: George Allen and Unwin, pp. 90–3.

The cultivated teacher

During the 1950s other branches of the teaching profession continued to have a very different entry route from that of the primary schools. The majority of teachers in independent schools had no professional training. The more prestigious the school, the more likely was it that the new teacher was directly recruited after a first degree from Oxford or Cambridge.[13] Sir Charles Morris, when Vice-Chancellor of Leeds University, claimed of university Education staff in 1960, 'Many headmasters and other senior schoolmasters – although not so many headmistresses – positively speak ill of them; the public schools, and perhaps the direct grant schools, do not, to say the least of it, give them any encouragement'.[14] If teacher training is a prerequisite for effective teaching, pupils of the most famous independent schools suffered educational disadvantage over many generations! Lionel Elvin did not think other heads much more supportive than those of the independent schools. He claimed that when headmasters 'get together in their conferences or sound off to the press they can almost always be relied on to damn the colleges without even faint praise'.[15]

Most entrants into teaching in secondary grammar schools under LEA control undertook, usually after a three year degree course, a year of teacher education in a university school or department of education, at the end of which they were awarded a Post-Graduate Certificate of Education (PGCE). Increasing numbers of PGCE holders in 'surplus' subjects, such as history and English, also entered secondary modern and secondary technical schools during the late 1950s, since there were insufficient posts for them all in grammar schools. Conversely, in 'shortage' subjects, such as mathematics and science, but also

---

13 For most men, of course, until 1959, two years of national service intervened between graduation and a career, or between leaving school and entering higher education. The disadvantaged female teachers did not enjoy this rich experience. They had some compensation in two years' earnings which were far higher than those of men conscripted into the armed forces, but this consideration never weakened feminist arguments about the evils of gender-differentiated salaries. See Geoffrey Partington (1976). *Women Teachers in England and Wales in the Twentieth Century*. Windsor: National Foundation for Educational Research.
14 Morris, Sir C. (1960). *The Universities and the Teaching Profession*. London: National Union of Teachers, p. 7 (cited in Taylor, 1969, p. 221).
15 Elvin, 1971, p. 17.

in specialist areas such as physical education, domestic science and handicrafts, many non-graduate certificated teachers gained posts in grammar schools. PGCE courses concentrated on teaching methods in the one or two subjects to be taught in the schools and specialist subject lecturers usually supervised teaching practice. Applicants for PGCE courses were chosen primarily, of course, on the basis of presumed adequacy in their main teaching subject(s), as attested by their degrees, but some efforts were usually made to ensure that those accepted were of good character. Such checks may often have been perfunctory, but they were certainly more strenuous than for entry to degree courses.

It was generally assumed that a university graduate had already mastered the content of the subject to be taught. This assumption was not always justified, since in some school subjects, such as history, it was very likely that large areas of school syllabuses had not been studied by PGCE students or beginning teachers since they were 11 or 12 years old. There were also courses in general educational ideas and during the 1950s more specialised courses were increasingly offered in philosophy of education, history of education, sociology of education and psychology of education/learning theory, often as options. Psychology of education was much more likely to be compulsory than history or sociology of education.

The prestige of PGCE courses was often scarcely higher within the universities themselves than Sir Charles Morris held it to be outside them. He placed among 'facts [that] are fairly clear', the fact that 'the professors and other university teachers in the primary university subjects have not themselves come to believe in the value of graduate training'. Lionel Elvin bemoaned in 1963 that until recently Education had been barely tolerated as part of universities.[16] William Taylor conceded in 1969 that 'Departments and Institutes of Education have tended to be small, inadequately staffed, badly housed and held in poor regard within the university and in the schools.'[17] Taylor held that negative images 'seem to be subscribed to and voiced by Education staff themselves as frequently as by colleagues in other subjects'.[18] A consideration which was more important,

---

16 Reported in *Universities Quarterly* (1963), 17 (2), p. 179 (cited in Taylor, 1969, p. 219).
17 Taylor, 1969, p. 219.
18 Taylor, 1969, p. 222.

although not mentioned by Taylor or Elvin, was that students enrolled in a PGCE usually found the university-based courses intellectually undemanding when compared with those in the final year of their honours degree which usually immediately preceded the PGCE, although many found teaching practice a severe challenge. Yet university Education lecturers were in something of a cleft stick. If they made their courses more intellectually demanding, as many did during the 1960s when the educational disciplines most flourished in ITT, they were accused by many teachers and many of their own students of being excessively theoretical and out of touch with the real needs of classrooms. If they failed to make their courses intellectually demanding, they continued to face accusations of providing 'soft options'.

During the 1960s there were major efforts to raise the academic level of courses in ITT, both in the colleges and universities. The basic ITT course in the colleges expanded in 1960 from two to three years and between 1960 and 1972 there was a three-fold increase in number of students enrolled. In 1963 the Robbins Committee recommended that ITT should be more closely integrated with other types of higher education. Robbins recommended a new degree, the Bachelor of Education (BEd), for college students held able to carry out degree work successfully, as the first step to an all-graduate teaching profession. It also recommended the transfer of power over the colleges from LEAs to new structures in which the universities would be the dominant force. The new structures which emerged, after LEA resistance had been overcome, were twenty Area Training Organisations (ATO), each based on a university wherever possible. The training colleges were renamed Colleges of Education and most soon expanded in size and became co-educational instead of single-sex institutions. Courses leading to careers other than teaching were offered, although teaching remained dominant in most cases.

Since the 1944 Education Act, which followed the recommendations of the McNair Report in this respect, the administrative control of the colleges had been jointly in the hands of the Ministry of Education (subsequently the DES), the LEAs and the college's own governors, with oversight of academic development in the hands of the university-based Institutes of Education. Most teacher educators resented the multiplicity of formal controls over their work, especially those exerted by

LEAs, but many were later to find equally irksome, first, extended university powers, especially those over the validation of the BEd, and, later, those of the DES as exercised through the TTA. Warnings of dangers to the independence of the colleges from university control had been raised by a significant minority of the McNair Committee, which favoured a joint-boards scheme which, they held, 'involves an association of equals in the discharge of a common task instead of making the training colleges dependent on the universities'. During the 1970s several colleges, with Bulmershe and Didsbury in the lead, were sufficiently alienated from university supervision to seek BEd accreditation from the newly created Council for National Academic Awards (CNAA). Other institutions of higher education which had recently entered ITT, such as North East London Polytechnic, sought CNAA validation from the beginning of their education degrees. However, the CNAA sometimes proved more demanding than the ATO and rejected some BEd proposals, notably from polytechnics, on the grounds of weakness in structure and inadequate qualifications among their academic staff.

The Robbins Report, as Eric Hoyle and Peter John of Bristol University School of Education have put it, 'gave scant attention to the practical training of teachers or to the relationship between theory and practice in the education curriculum'. Hoyle and John added, 'Perhaps its most significant effect was the strengthening of the academic subjects'.[19] The Plowden Report, despite its predilection for child-centred methods of teaching, followed the same path and urged that the central role of academic subject studies in BEd courses should be the furtherance of the personal development of student teachers, since once they started teaching they would have less opportunity 'for the systematic study of a subject for its own sake'. Brian Ellis of the University of Warwick Institute of Education has observed that such academic courses 'were often unrelated to the fact that the students were training to teach'.[20] Indeed, the Plowden Report specifically urged that such courses should 'not be

---

19 Hoyle, E. and John, P. (1998). 'Teacher Education: the Prime Subject' in *Oxford Review of Education,* 24 (1), p. 73.
20 Ellis, B. (1995). 'Rethinking the Nature of Subject Studies in Primary Initial Teacher Education' in *British Journal of Educational Studies,* XXXIII (2), p. 147.

related to the day to day work of primary schools'. It would be unfair to the Plowden Committee to suggest that its members rejected the importance of character or practical teaching skills; it is more likely that they simply assumed that these goods would adequately be fostered, provided that standards of scholarship were raised. If that was the case, it was an unwarranted assumption.

A significant, and perhaps unintended, effect of Robbins and Plowden was to change the reference group to which most college of education lecturers looked most eagerly for legitimisation. In the past they had sought approval mainly from teachers in schools where their students carried out teaching practice. After the Robbins and Plowden Reports, college lecturers looked increasingly for approval to university Education academics. Before the 1960s many college lecturers held strongly that their own courses were a better preparation for teaching than those of the universities: one argument was that the single PGCE year was insufficient to initiate entrants adequately into the ethos of teaching; another was that university lecturers were usually too theoretical and intellectual, even though the rest of the university might consider them insufficiently so. In their turn, to be sure, college lecturers were often considered over-theoretical and impractical by teachers in the schools, some of whom also thought the college lecturers had found a more leisured and less demanding way of life than that of the regular classroom. However, the old college staff usually had considerable experience in the schools in which their students were to teach, even if the time gap inevitably widened with the years.

The massive expansion of the 1960s meant that large numbers of new college lecturers had to be appointed in both substantive curriculum subjects and educational disciplines. In only a few cases was it possible to find staff who had considerable experience in schools, particularly primary schools, yet were also sufficiently well qualified academically to satisfy universities that they could teach to degree level. Sometimes, in order to teach the educational disciplines, established college staff were sent to universities for one year courses, but it was not always easy for old dogs to learn new tricks and it was rare for them after their return to college to feel able to discuss matters of scholarship on equal terms with the university lecturers who had taught them on secondment. In substantive subjects there were rather more capable scholars who were also experienced teachers, although few were of comparable academic standing to university lecturers in the same disciplines. The increase in the number of teacher educators also led to a massive shift in gender-balance. In 1938 the staff of training colleges in England and Wales consisted of 515 women and 181 men, and relative proportions were similar in 1954 (1625 women and 671 men), but after the rapid expansion of the late 1950s and early 1960s there were 2665 women and 4027 men in the colleges of education.[21] Although some old 'mother-hens' were male, the large majority were female, and although some of the new specialists in academic subjects and the disciplines of education were female, a huge majority were male.

The changes of the 1960s resulted in the marginalisation of the once central role of the education tutor. In so far as any college of education staff had major influence over students' thinking under the new order, it was likely to be those who were substantive subject specialists or authorities in a discipline of education. With increasing choices of courses on offer, few of the new teacher educators were able to exert the same amount of personal influence over their students as had the old training college staff. This no doubt had its advantages, especially as the students usually had the opportunity to experience a wider range of informed judgements on contestable educational questions, but it became more difficult for student-teachers to form a clear and coherent concept of the role of the teacher.

Factional rivalries were common within the colleges in the 1960s and 1970s. Three groups were in competition for course time and professional advancement. The former training college lecturers mainly survived in professional methods courses, but they were increasingly distanced from the two new types of appointee: scholars in substantive subjects and experts in educational disciplines. When I was appointed as a history lecturer at Doncaster College of Education in 1966, I also gave a course in history of education within the college's Education department, whose members conducted tutorials based on my lectures. As I had taught for twelve years in secondary schools but had hardly even entered a primary school since I was eleven, the old Education hands could have been scathing about supervision of primary school teaching practice being undertaken by me and

---

21 See Taylor, 1969, ch. 8: pp. 202 ff.

many others equally unqualified to give significant help in primary classrooms, but most of the Education staff were instead very willing to give me advice. As a result I spent quite a lot of time with them. In perhaps my second term, the Head of the History Department took me on one side and admonished me as follows: 'Partington! [she used surnames only for most of her colleagues]. Please remember that you are a member of the history department here. You spend too much time over coffee with those education people. They are only a lot of old primary heads, you know'. At Coventry College of Education I was a member of the Education department and soon found that I was on the wrong side of the line in the eyes of some of the history lecturers.

Yet there can be no doubt that average academic standards achieved in the colleges of education by the late 1960s were far higher than those in the former training colleges a decade earlier. Just before the rapid expansion of the new universities, larger numbers of students with good A-levels entered the colleges than in the past. It was this reduction in the old gap which made the continuation of the 'binary divide' increasingly obnoxious to many teacher educators, to teacher unions, which saw higher professional prestige in a unified system of teacher education, and to many Whitehall and LEA administrators, who in general preferred uniformity to diversity in education at any level.

The general temper of educational theory was still tolerant and pluralist. David Carr of the Faculty of Education of Heriot-Watt University recently described the approach of the standard bearers of academic philosophy of education, Richard Peters and Paul Hirst, as 'by today's standards' an 'extremely broad and liberal conception of teacher education, focused upon initiation into a range of reasonably reputable academic studies and disciplines of defensible relevance to education'. Sociologists of education such as Brian Davies and William Taylor, historians of education such as Harry Armytage and Kenneth Charlton, and educational psychologists such as H. J. Butcher and Stephen Wiseman, could also be relied upon to present a scholarly and fair account of conflicting views in their own disciplines, however strongly each might be committed to a specific position. However, as David Carr has noted, 'to a large extent the subsequent history of training for teaching is a story of increasing disenchantment with this ambitious academic faculty based conception of professional understanding dreamed up in the heady days of sixties educational expansion'.[22]

Much subsequent disenchantment with ITT had its roots less in rejection of the Hirst–Peters emphasis on the importance of educational ideas than in the inability of HEIs to cope with frequent organisational changes. Although teacher education remained the staple business of most colleges of education during the 1960s and early 1970s, the existence of even a few courses entirely unconnected with preparation for teaching weakened the traditions inherited from the training colleges. This trend was enhanced by the publication in 1972 by the Department of Education and Science (DES) of *Teacher Education and Training*, known widely as the James Report after its chairman, Lord James of Rusholme, Vice-Chancellor of the University of York and formerly High Master of Manchester Grammar School. The James Report condemned the old monotechnic tradition which survived in most of the colleges of education, even though some offered non-teaching courses.

As a headmaster, Eric James had, when it was fully legal so to do, recruited Manchester Grammar teachers from first-class honours graduates who had not availed themselves of a PGCE. He was not an admirer of much educational theorising, any more than were the former training college lecturers, whose professional backgrounds were so very different from his. If there had to be professional training for teachers, James was determined it should be directly related to what schools believed was needed. The James Committee demanded of initial teacher education that its courses should be 'unashamedly specialised and functional' and 'sharply focused' and 'its objectives specified as precisely as possible'. It doubted whether the educational disciplines were even 'a useful major element in initial training', although a grudging concession was made that they might be 'seen as contributory to effective teaching', provided that they reformed themselves. Its insistence on greater immediate relevance of educational studies to classroom teaching to some extent anticipated 'New Right' critiques of the 1980s, but the James Report had very different outcomes from those of Conservative policies a decade later.

---

22 Carr, D. (1997). 'The Uses of Literacy in Teacher Education' in *British Journal of Educational Studies*, 45 (1), p. 55.

In the aftermath of James main subjects were often taught in a large and complex institution by lecturers who had no special interest or experience in teacher education, let alone in educational theories. This reversal of fortunes for the recent arrivals who had been appointed to teach the educational disciplines was bliss to some of the veterans of training college days, but the old order did not return and the refuge of the old guard sometimes became pedagogy with a functionalist rather than a child-centred emphasis, offered in courses with names such as 'Geography in Education', or 'Early Childhood Mathematical Experiences'.[23] However, the main single cause for growing malaise in ITT during the late 1960s and the 1970s was not rapid organisational changes, disruptive as many of them were, or in tensions between the old college and university traditions or between the competing claims of generic classroom skills, main subject knowledge related mainly to 'personal' development, teaching the school curriculum, and the disciplines of education, sharp as those often were. The most potent source of malaise, scarcely mentioned by Carr and entirely absent from the James Report, was the establishment of radical ideological influence over much of teacher education.

The teacher as transformer of society

During the periods in which the concepts of the teacher as promoter of civic virtue or as scholar were dominant in teacher education in Britain, there were always teacher educators, as well as teachers, whose prime concern with education was that it should contribute to the radical reconstruction of what they conceived to be an unjust capitalist society. However, in the pre-1960s many on the Old Left were in harmony with important themes in the old training college tradition and/or sympathised with the new thrust for more scholarly teachers, so that sharp disagreements between Old Left lecturers and the colleagues about methods of work were rare.

The Old Left had a long history of seeking to improve moral standards and civility among children from social strata who seemed conspicuously lacking in these qualities. Leading figures in English radical traditions, such as William Cobbett, Robert

---

23 Bell, A. (1981). 'Social Relationships in Teacher Education' in *British Journal of Sociology of Education*, 2 (1), p. 18.

Own, Francis Place, Thomas Cooper, William Lovett and many other Chartists, F. D. Maurice and many other Christian Socialists, George Odger, Robert Applegarth and many other Trade Union leaders, Keir Hardie and others in the Independent Labour Party, had placed great faith in education as much as a means of moral upliftment of the masses as of their material advancement. In 1926 G. D. H. Cole was typical in his confidence that, since 1900, 'General elementary education, of course, had made a huge difference to manners, habits and social outlook' among the working-classes.[24] Cole related the fact that 'the working-class consumption of alcohol greatly decreased' to education having 'greatly improved in both quantity and quality'. He added that 'with the growth of education went a rapid spread of culture, and a great extension of the reading public'.[25] In playful mood in *Pygmalion* Bernard Shaw placed the 'undeserving' dustman Doolittle above the 'deserving' poor, but Shaw was well aware of the dire effects in working-class districts of domestic violence, promiscuity, drunkenness and gambling, and hoped that universal education would help to reduce vice.

Similar views were widely shared by the more revolutionary elements of the Old Left. Some of Karl Marx's own most powerful thunder was reserved for the *lumpenproletariat*, feckless and demoralised elements of the poor on whom no reliance could ever be placed. Hard work and self-discipline were highly prized by the Italian communist, Antonio Gramsci, who wrote

> In education one is dealing with children in whom one has to inculcate certain habits of diligence, precision, poise (even physical poise), ability to concentrate upon specific subjects, which cannot be acquired without the mechanical repetition of disciplined and methodical acts ... It is also true that it will always be an effort to learn physical self-discipline and self-control; the pupil has in effect to undergo a psycho-physical training. Many people have to be persuaded that studying too is a job, and a very tiring one, with its own particular apprenticeship – involving muscles and nerves as well as intellect. It is a process of adaptation, a habit acquired with effort, tedium and

---

24 Cole, G. D. H. (1926). *A Short History of the British Working Class Movement. vol II,* London: George Allen and Unwin, p. 194.
25 ibid, *vol III,* p. 223.

even suffering. If one wishes to produce scholars, one has to start at this point and apply pressure throughout the educational system in order to succeed in creating those thousands or hundreds or only dozens of scholars of the highest quality who are necessary to every great civilization.[26]

In their desire to extend to the masses significant knowledge previously confined to cultural elites or privileged minorities, many on the Old Left found common ground with liberal educators. This reformist Old Left, as well as Marx, understood that truth and knowledge could be and often had been and still were distorted to suit material or ideological interests, but they also accepted with Marx that objective knowledge could be established once ideological distortions were corrected. They would have agreed with Gramsci that it is a 'simple and fundamental fact that there exist objective intractable laws to which man must adapt if he is to master them in his turn'.[27] They did not wish to confine working-class children to even the best version of 'working-class culture': the Chartist schools of the mid-nineteenth century had sought to give working-class children access to Shakespeare and Milton, not to peasant or proletarian literature, and to the best science of the day.

The 1950s case against secondary selection and for comprehensive education was based on the claim that it was unfair to exclude children in secondary modern and technical schools from the academic curriculum and liberal knowledge. The Old Left generally wanted to make such a curriculum more widely available, not to end it. In a euphoric moment, Hugh Gaitskell claimed that comprehensive schools meant 'a grammar school education for all'. Ellen Wilkinson was not ashamed to express an ambition to see Britain become a 'Third Programme society' – one in which high culture was accessible to the mass of the people. Most of the early comprehensive schools of the 1950s, especially those of the London County Council, sought to extend a version of the classical-humanist curriculum to far larger numbers of students than in the past. Charges, such as those made by Geoffrey Bantock, that they were merely offering a

---

26 Gramsci, A. (1971). *Selections from the Prison Notebooks* (ed. and trans. Q. Hoare & G. N. Smith). London: New Left Books, pp. 37, 42.
27 Gramsci, 1971, p. 34.

'watered-down' grammar school curriculum unsuited to the needs and interests of most working-class pupils, were rejected as reactionary and groundless.

Many on the Old Left who had little political sympathy with the Soviet Union considered that its educational achievements showed that a demanding curriculum could be extended on a wider scale than hitherto thought possible. In 1919, when some Bolsheviks sought to expunge 'bourgeois culture' from the curriculum of the new Soviet schools and replace it with 'Prolecult', Lenin replied that 'Proletarian culture must be the result of the natural development of the stores of knowledge which mankind has accumulated under the yoke of capitalist society, Landlord society and bureaucratic society' and argued that 'the tuition, training and education of the youth must be based on the material that was bequeathed to us by the old society'.[28] As a result, despite its deformation by indoctrination, Soviet education was to offer a broad scientific-humanistic curriculum.

Brian and Joan Simon, two leading British communist educationists, claimed that Soviet educational achievements were taking place within 'what is basically a non-streamed common school system'.[29] 'Basically' is, of course, an elastic term and, as the Simons noted, Soviet education had developed 'methods of diagnosis and selection for special schools which finds a reflection in the detailed and careful procedure followed before any child is classified as mentally retarded and recommended for transfer'.[30] There was an elaborate system of special treatment for children with learning difficulties, as well as boarding schools for children, especially those of isolated ethnic minorities, living in environments with very limited cognitive stimulation, and others for children thought to be of exceptional potentiality in several activities. Soviet schools placed considerable pressure on children who were failing to 'keep up': they organised peer-group pressure through the Young Pioneers and other state-sponsored organisations of youth, and required extra school

---

28 Lenin, V. I. (1943). *Selected Works XI*. Moscow: Foreign Languages Publishing House, pp. 484, 468.
29 Simon, B. and Simon, J. (1963). *Educational Psychology in the USSR*. London: Routledge and Kegan Paul, p. vii.
30 Simon and Simon, 1963, p. 6 (the procedure mentioned is described in A. L. Luria & G. M. Dulnev, *Principles Governing the Selection of Children for Special Schools*. Moscow, 1956).

attendance during 'normal' vacations. However, given these reservations and admitting that its statistics might well have been highly unreliable, reports about Soviet education encouraged reasonable hopes that mass education of a high intellectual standard could be achieved. Indeed, it is fair to argue that the Soviet system failed not because of, but in spite of, its educational system, which made available a huge cadre of highly educated graduates for the command economy and the central plan.

There was considerable overlap between the Old Left and the social missionary and scholarly strands in teacher education on issues concerning intelligence and the relative influence of heredity and environment on educational achievement. Cyril Burt, the first educational psychologist appointed in Britain, received his knighthood from the Attlee Labour Government and was well regarded then by many on the Old Left. Burt demonstrated that many children previously classified as ineducable were in fact merely victims of adverse environmental conditions and that conventional achievement tests, even when coupled with teachers' observations, often failed to pick out working-class children with high intellectual potential. His IQ tests were designed to identify such children. Burt wrote:

> Attainment is a poor measure of capacity, and ignorance no proof of defect. Merely from school work, neither normal endowment nor abnormal, neither high nor low, can conclusively be inferred ... To suppose that wherever attainments are meagre, ability must also be weak, will always be fallacious. Poor health, poor homes, irregular attendance, lack of interest, want of will – these are far commoner as causes of inability to spell or calculate than are inherent weakness of intellect and genuine defect of mind. Certainly, the dull are usually backward; but the backward are not necessarily dull ... Even with average children, the amount and accuracy of their present knowledge forms but a rough and uncertain index of their power to acquire more knowledge.[31]

However, Burt insisted that even more variance in intelligence was attributable to genetic than environmental influences, adducing evidence from wide variation in intelligence and

---

31 Burt, C. (1962). *Mental and Scholastic Tests*. London: Staples Press, pp. 1–4.

attainment among children in total or near-total institutions, such as orphanages in which no concessions are made to their individuality, and from the higher correlation in intelligence between identical compared with fraternal twins of the same sex, although each child experienced the same environment as its twin in most cases of both identical and merely fraternal pairs. Within a year of Burt's death, he was attacked as a charlatan, even though his findings were entirely consistent with those of every other serious psychometrician. In 1997 I found no course materials or recommended texts in ITT in institutions I visited which acknowledged Burt's great services to education, even though alarm was being widely expressed about possible abuses of genetic cloning, alarm which only makes sense if inherited characteristics are of great importance.

Virtually every teacher educator in the early 1950s, including the Old Left, also had a favourable attitude towards tests and examinations. Like the pioneers of competitive examinations for entry to the Civil Service in Britain, they regarded an efficient examination system as the best alternative to nepotism and corruption, a position supported by Gramsci, who did not doubt that testing could be carried out in a fair and objective manner even in Fascist Italy. Gramsci suggested that his nephew's first public exam marked 'his entry into manly society' and he assured his son that regular testing would 'make it easier to see how you are getting on in general'.[32]

The child-centred teacher

In nineteenth-century Britain almost all the teaching which could in any way be described as child-centred took place in independent schools, and in only a very few of them, usually those for younger children. The first major critic of traditional pedagogy from within the state system of education was Edmond Holmes in his 1911 *What Is and What Might Be*. Since Holmes had been the Board of Education's Chief Inspector for Elementary Schools, his impassioned claim that 'Blind, passive, literal, unintelligent obedience is the basis on which the whole

---

32 Gramsci, A. (1974). *Letters from Prison* (trans. H. Hamilton). New Edinburgh Review: Special Numbers on Gramsci, Letter CXC. See Entwistle H. (1979). *Antonio Gramsci: Conservative Schooling for Radical Politics*. London: Routledge & Kegan Paul.

system of Western education has been reared' gained widespread attention.³³ Holmes influenced some lecturers in the recently created university departments of education and rather more in the training colleges, especially among lecturers responsible for early childhood education. In 1924 Lance Jones claimed that in such courses could be found 'more appreciation of new ideas and movements' than in any other part of education in Britain.³⁴ Leading figures included Percy Nunn, Godfrey Thomson, C. W. Valentine, J. J. Findlay, Constance Bloor, Nancy Catty, W. G. Sleight, Lillian de Lissa, Susan Isaacs and John Adams. The most influential books produced by them were probably Nunn's *Education: Its Data and First Principles* (Arnold, 1920) and various works by Susan Isaacs, appointed in 1933 as head of the newly formed Department of Child Development in the London University Institute of Education, where Nunn was Director.³⁵ Lillian de Lissa, principal of Gipsy Hill Training College and a leader in the Froebelian Kindergarten movement, was highly energetic in propagating child-centred education. Thus it was not surprising that the 1931 *Report of the Consultative Committee to the Board of Education on the Primary School* urged that the junior school curriculum should be considered in terms 'of activity and experience rather than knowledge to be acquired or facts to be stored', and made favourable references to the work of Rachel and Margaret Macmillan and Maria Montessori. In some religious foundations transcendental educational ideas were beginning to blend with child-centred beliefs, particularly among 'Froebel-trained' lecturers, although such tendencies were weak in the Roman Catholic training colleges.

Although prominent child-centred thinkers exerted a powerful influence on some training college lecturers, most of whatever effect was transmitted to student-teachers seems to have waned rapidly once the latter took up teaching posts. As late as the 1960s Marten Shipman found that, although 'students held very progressive views while in college, regardless of

---

33 Holmes, E. (1911). *What Is and What Might Be*. London: Constable, p. 50.
34 Jones, L. (1924). *The Training of Teachers in England and Wales*. London: Constable, p. 157.
35 See Isaacs, S. (1930). *Intellectual Growth in Young Children*. London: Routledge; (1932). *The Children We Teach*. London: University of London Press; and (1933). *Social Development in Young Children*. London: Routledge.

whether they were primary or secondary', they soon 'moved in the traditional direction to hold identical views to the staff of the type of school in which they were teaching'.[36] This failure to exert continued influence may partly have stemmed from the failure of many child-centred college lecturers to practice what they preached. It was sometimes a matter of 'do what I say' rather than 'do what I do'. Geoffrey Bantock wrote of 'those splendid old battle-axes who are rigid for freedom and never permit the students to question the orthodoxy of the permissiveness they are to take into the schools'.[37] A more sympathetic critic, the Australian historian of education Richard Selleck, noted similarly that 'crowded rooms of would-be teachers often listened to lectures bemoaning the inefficiency of lessons to large classes, and students solemnly copied out notes from lectures which extolled "activity" methods'.[38] Strict limitations usually remained on the degree of permissiveness in even the most child-centred of the training colleges of the 1950s, and pioneers such as Susan Isaacs, Percy Nunn and Maria Montessori combined inculcation of a strong core of basic knowledge with their advocacy of greater discovery and inquiry in the classroom. Their ideas had little in common with most of the post-1960 New Left versions of child-centred education.

However, after 1945, starting with early childhood education, there was, despite the limitations noted by Marten Shipman, a greater willingness among newly qualified teachers to apply in their own classrooms some of the child-centred methods advocated in ITT. The publication of the Plowden Report in 1967 marked a new high point in the prestige of child-centred ideas in teacher education, especially in early childhood and primary teaching. Key child-centred ideas endorsed by Plowden included that children have 'natures' which will 'develop naturally' if only teachers will create the appropriate 'natural' environments, in whose creation 'sensitivity and observation are called for rather

---

36 Shipman, M. D. (1966). *Personal and Social Influences on the Work of a Teachers' Training College.* Unpublished Ph.D. thesis, University of London, p. 263 (cited in Taylor, 1969, p. 277).
37 Bantock, G. H. (1970). 'Conflicts of Values in Teacher Education' in C. B. Cox and A. E. Dyson (eds). *Black Paper Three: Goodbye Mr Short.* London: the Critical Quarterly Society, p. 113.
38 Selleck, R. J. W. (1972). *English Primary Education and the Progressives, 1914–1939.* London: Routledge & Kegan Paul, p. 121.

than intervention from the teacher'.[39] The Plowden Report held that knowledge cannot, or perhaps should not, be divided into separate compartments and that children's self-chosen activities within an integrated curriculum should be encouraged. Plowden's emphasis was on the teacher as a guide and arranger of the learning environment, not an as instructor, and creativity was conceived as a generic faculty which might well be damaged by close specification of rules in writing, drawing or composing. The Plowden Committee was reluctant to concede that a considerable amount of information has to be imparted to children which few, if any, can possibly discover for themselves. In ITT the Plowden doctrines required open-plan infant schools, unstreamed primary classes, topic and theme-based curricula, group-activities and individualised programmes in place of class teaching, and 'learning-readiness'. Greater emphasis on children's own activity and a reduction in the excessive didacticism of some traditional classrooms were to be welcomed, but one good way of learning some things very rapidly became a new dogma applied to learning all things.

---

[39] Plowden Report (1967). *Children and their Primary Schools*. London: Central Advisory Council for Education (England), para. 527.

2 | Ideological Capture by the New Left

By ideological capture I mean that an unduly limited range of ideas is presented as though it represented the only morally or intellectually tenable view, and that contrary ideas are ignored or grossly distorted. Ideological hegemony was established over much of teacher education in the 1960s and 1970s by New Left radical-reconstructionists, who based themselves largely on neo-Marxist doctrines, with some additions from child-centred thought. A good example of the way in which New Left thinking came to permeate teacher education is the title of an article by John Hull of the University of Birmingham School of Education: 'Religious Education in the State Schools in Late Capitalist Societies'.[40] Hull, himself a religious educator, did not hold New Left views, but he must have assumed, like the crowd who gazed at the Emperor's new clothes, that his vociferous colleagues in Birmingham University's Centre for Contemporary Cultural Studies knew something he did not. At the very time Hull was writing several states were becoming late or former Marxist societies, whereas the society in which he lived, and those like it, were still, so far as we can tell, in their prime.

The New Left and civic virtue

The New Left differed sharply from their predecessors in their view of the role of teachers as moral agents. Neo-Marxism scoffed at any ideas which smacked of 'social control' or 'gentling the masses'. Douglas Holly, of Leicester University School of Education, could not stomach the claim implicit in the subtitle of Harold Entwistle's book on Gramsci: 'Conservative Education for Radical Politics'. Holly accused Entwistle of having joined

---

40 Hull, J. M. (1990), 'Religious Education in State Schools in Late Capitalist Societies' in *British Journal of Educational Studies*, XXXVIII (4), pp. 335–348.

the 'apologists for bourgeois property relations' and of falsely representing Gramsci as a defender of 'deference to authority, acceptance of received opinion, subservience to imposed "standards"'.[41] Holly was appalled that Entwistle 'chooses to represent him [Gramsci] as recommending for the young the moral necessity of work'. There was no likelihood of Holly or other neo-Marxists making any such recommendation, nor of their urging British schoolchildren to become 'good pupils of a bourgeois education system greedily consuming as much knowledge as they can lay their hands on', Holly's perverse depiction of Entwistle's position.

Nell Keddie of the Open University insisted that all cultures have equal validity, so that there could be no culturally superior curriculum, any more than there could be such a thing as cultural deprivation. Keddie claimed that all children, however culturally deprived they might appear to outsiders, could not be other than 'experienced participants in a way of life that has its own validity'.[42] Keddie's apparently egalitarian denial of the very existence of cultural deprivation stood in sharp contrast to Engels' indignation in his 1844 *Condition of the Working Class in England* against cultural and material deprivation. If Keddie had read *Animal Farm,* she had not understood one of its most famous phrases: 'all are equal, but some are more equal than others'. Although she proclaimed all cultures as of equal value, the culture of 'unprivileged' or 'underprivileged' pupils was superior in her eyes to that of their presumably 'overprivileged' teachers. Keddie urged student teachers and young teachers to learn from their students, not to try to impose on them middle-class behaviour and irrelevant academic lore.

Another influential figure in rejecting the values of the old 'civil religion' held by many of the Old Left was Paul Willis, initially prominent in Birmingham University's Centre for Cultural Studies and later an educational adviser to the Wolverhampton local authority. Willis' *Learning to Labour* is in large part a study of alienated working-class boys, the 'lads', who

---

41 Holly, D. (1980). Review of Harold Entwistle (1979). *Antonio Gramsci: Conservative Education for Radical Politics* in *British Journal of Sociology of Education,* 1 (3), p. 315.
42 See Keddie, N. (1973). 'Introduction' to Keddie, N. (ed). *Tinker, Tailor ... the Myth of Cultural Deprivation.* Harmondsworth: Penguin.

despise 'ear-holes', boys who work hard in school. Willis seemed to share their contempt of 'conformist' students, portrayed by him as 'timid sheep who sometimes, when the teacher allows classroom disorder to erupt, indignantly remind the shepherd of his duty'. One of the 'lads', when asked 'Why not be like the ear 'oles, why not try to get CSEs?' replied, 'What will they have to look back on? sitting in a classroom sweating their b ... off, you know, while we've been fighting the Pakis, fighting the JAs (Jamaicans). Some of the things we've done on teachers! It'll be a laff when we look back on it'.[43]

There had been much more real poverty in Britain in the 1920s and 1930s than in the 1960s and 1970s. Many Old Left teachers had been personally active in helping to relieve hardship among their pupils and their families, but they did not excuse bad conduct as the fault of adverse social conditions. It was partly to the credit of the schools that the depression years, or the years of war, did not lead to a massive increase in crime. Indeed, nineteenth-century trends towards greater civility and honesty continued during those dark times. Too many New Left teacher educators failed to recognise the positive value of what the schools had done. Instead, they disparaged the schools as agents of unjust social control. The New Left held that criminal activity was created by poverty or sickness over which offenders had little or no control. Student teachers were assured that all punishment, not merely corporal varieties, are in principle wrong. What was required of teachers was not to be judgemental but to seek social justice which would transform young offenders into followers of the light. It was not very surprising that classrooms became increasingly unstable and the task of the teacher ever more onerous. Rates of stress and strain increased among teachers, including head teachers who were taking early retirement in unprecedented numbers.

The New Left and liberal knowledge

Whereas the Old Left and earlier Marxists thought it possible to perceive bias created by material and ideological interests and thus to establish objective truths and reliable knowledge, neo-Marxism denied that human reason had this potentiality. 'Knowledge' was often placed in sneer quotes. Michael F. D.

---

[43] Willis, P. (1977). *Learning to Labour*. Farnborough, Saxon House, p. 188.

Young of the London University Institute of Education, in a book which became wellnigh ubiquitous in reading lists for ITT courses during the 1970s, targeted for attack what he called 'a new absolutism, that of science and reason'.[44] Young claimed that all attempts to 'distinguish home from school, learning from play, academic from non-academic, and "able" or "bright" from "dull" or "stupid", must be conceived as socially constructed, with some in a position to impose their constructions or meanings on others'.[45] Of course, there must be a stipulative element in distinguishing academic from non-academic or clever people from dull ones, and so on; and some social structure must exist before the roles of pupil and teacher can be undertaken. But it is false that these distinctions are *only* social constructs, in the sense of meanings imposed by the strong on the weak.[46] Such distinctions as that between dull and clever people are necessarily made in all human societies and it does student teachers little good to assure them that every such distinction can only be merely arbitrary. Unfortunately, during the 1970s the fallacy of *'only* socially constructed' became the stock-in-trade of whole tribes of 'radical constructivists' who came to dominate science and maths methodology in ITT in Britain and much of the English-speaking world.

As allies on the epistemological front neo-Marxists recruited a range of relativists who held that bias arising from material and ideological interests was less important than an inescapable subjectivity which, they considered, arises from our inability to observe or judge from more than one position at a time. Allies were also secured among some child-centred educationists who contended that school knowledge not directly based on pupils' own experiences and interests was likely to prove beyond their understanding, or boring or irrelevant even if they could understand it.

Neo-Marxists held with Antony Arblaster that

> ... neutrality, or impartiality, in the sense of a demand that teacher and students do not take sides and do not allow interpretation or

---

44 Young, M. F. D. (ed) (1971). *Knowledge and Control: New Directions in the Sociology of Education.* London: Collier-Macmillan, p. 3.
45 Young, 1971, p. 2.
46 See Flew, A. (1976). *Sociology, Equality and Education.* London: Macmillan, pp. 22 ff.

opinion (or bias or prejudice – call it what you will) to contaminate the pure stream is an absurdity.[47]

They endorsed the view of Kevin Harris, an Australian teacher educator, who claimed that 'there cannot be a-political knowledge about anything, nor can there be a-political production, selection and transmission of knowledge'. In addition, Harris held, 'all research, in the sense of practical activity within social-historical contexts (which would necessarily include scientific research) is political ... there is thus simply no argument about the political nature of educational research – and there is simply no argument about the political nature of scientific research, since in so far as research can be scientific at all it must, being research, be political anyway.'[48] Such claims were asserted as dogma, revealed as truth to New Left believers, even though some, including Harris, were happy on occasion to cite in support of some of their own arguments research which, he implied, was impartial, objective and non-political.

Clive Harber and Roland Meighan of the Faculty of Education, University of Birmingham, explained that their students 'wrote their own syllabus, selected teaching methods, shared the tasks of teaching and organising course sessions, located appropriate resources and evaluated the outcomes'.[49] They described their operation as 'a case of democratic learning', perhaps to be contrasted with authoritarian or fascist practices elsewhere. One day is picked out for detailed description, beginning with 'The next day was devoted to a detailed and intense discussion of three themes of the hidden curriculum debate – race, class and gender – and to practical classroom strategies for dealing with these issues'. Then, 'towards the end of this session, and following a discussion of the neo-Marxist critique of education [spontaneously introduced no doubt by the ardent students], one student again raised the role of the tutors. This was not so much that the tutors were saying too much [perish the thought],

---

47 Arblaster, A. (1974). *Academic Freedom.* Harmondsworth: Penguin Educational, p. 17.
48 Harris, K. (1988). 'The Politics of Educational Research: From a Philosopher's Point of View' in *Educational Research and Perspectives,* 15 (2), pp. 26–7.
49 Harber, C. and Meighan, R. (1986). 'A Case of Democratic Learning in Teacher Education' in *Educational Review,* 38 (3), p. 273.

rather than too much authority was attached to what they said'.[50] Supports to the course included 'a visitor from the Birmingham Young Volunteers Social Education Project who talked on the role of BYV in fostering social education through Active Tutorial Work in Birmingham schools.' The ten references given by Harber and Meighan, excluding works of their own, included works by Paulo Freire, Ivan Illich, John Watts of Countesthorpe Comprehensive School (2) and Patricia White. Geoff Whitty and Michael F. D. Young entreated that their work should 'not be treated as a body of knowledge to be learned for a degree or a diploma' but 'as a meaningful contribution to efforts being made in a whole variety of contexts to create a socialist future'.[51]

The New Left and child-centred education

The New Left would not have gained its ascendancy in teacher education without seeing to be sympathetic to some child-centred ideas, such as hostility to teachers as agents of an alien authority and apparent acceptance of students as best judges of their own educational interests. Intense opposition to competitive examinations, or any other sorts of assessment, which revealed to the world significant individual or group differences and hostility to homework were important components of the new alliance between radical-reconstructionists and child-centred educators. Hatred, not only of 'league tables' but of external examinations of any character, became endemic in teacher unions as the influence of the New Left increased, although if no teachers can be shown to be of less than average competence, then none can be shown to be of superior ability and effectiveness either. There was a modicum of rationality in the unions' stance, since they were especially concerned with protecting their weakest members, however much their colleagues, just as likely to be union members, suffered along with the pupils from the incompetence of others. Yet it was entirely self-destructive for teacher educators to insist that schools made little or no difference to children's educational progress. However, just as many secondary teachers refused to criticise publicly primary schools whose students at the age of eleven were well below the standard

---

50 Harber & Meighan, 1986, p. 279.
51 Whitty, G. and Young M. F. D. (eds) (1976). *Explorations in the Politics of Educational Knowledge*. Driffield, Nafferton Books, p. 5.

reasonably to be expected, many higher education lecturers were loathe openly to criticise defaulting secondary schools, although complaints were made often enough behind closed doors. In public it was deemed better to concentrate on protests against the devotion of inadequate resources to education.

The New Left alliance elevated learning by doing over more purely cerebral activity. Rousseau himself had, of course, combined admiration for the unspoiled child as against the adult corrupted by society, with reverence for the 'noble savage' as against flawed European sophistication. The New Left publicly admired 'Third World' cultures as against western capitalism, as well as placing the supposed interests of children above the oppressive demands of formal knowledge. An intense dislike of the mainstream national culture the New Left had inherited became the driving force in 'anti-racism' programmes and in history syllabuses.

The amalgam of the 1970s emphasised the supposed interests of children as a peer group, rather than those of each individual child. John Dewey, although he also had a collectivist streak, wrote in 1899:

> The old education ... may be summed up by stating that the center of gravity is outside the child. It is in the teacher, the textbook, anywhere and everywhere you please except in the immediate instincts and activities of the child himself ... Now the change which is coming into education is the shifting of the center of gravity ... the child becomes the sun about which they are organised.[52]

Instead the New Left stereotyped children by groups, as 'working-class' children, 'Black' children, or females. Among the important neglected elements in child-centred ideas were the great emphasis once placed on the creative value of a distinctive 'world of childhood', in which traditional games and songs played an important part, and the works of writers such as the Grimms, Hans Anderson, Lewis Carroll and Kenneth Grahame. Instead, New Left radicalism gave children's everyday experiences outside the school a much greater part in school curricula than in the past.

---

52 Dewey, J. (1959). *School and Society*. Chicago: Phoenix Books, University of Chicago Press edition, p. 34.

Piaget urged the importance of maturation and growth, stages of development and learning readiness, but he had been vitally concerned with how to overcome obstacles to rapid learning. In contrast, the New Left constantly warned of dangers to children's self-esteem if in school they met challenges in which success is not guaranteed. One of the few pieces of educational research that a young teacher could be expected to know about in the 1970s was the work of Robert Rosenthal and Leonie Jacobson on the importance of high expectancy among parents and teachers.[53] Unfortunately, the lesson most education students derived from this was that children from disadvantaged backgrounds should not be confronted with difficult tasks and should never be told that they have failed. This 'Good boy, Leroy!' syndrome, as I termed it after witnessing its doleful effect on West Indian boys in London in particular, was based on low expectations and helped to widen group disparities in educational achievement. At soccer and other games boys were given a realistic appraisal of their talents, but in the classroom the anti-racist teacher had to preserve them from self-knowledge. It was fortunate for English sport that games coaches did not have to take courses in New Left educational theory.

There are several explanations for the apparent ease with which the New Left gained such a grip on teacher education during the late 1960s and the 1970s. One is that the organisational structure of the colleges was in constant turmoil, no less under the Wilson and Callaghan Labour governments than under the Conservatives. New Left activists often took a prominent part in opposing 'cuts' and various changes unpopular with most of their colleagues. This strengthened the view that, although neo-Marxist educational theory might seem 'extreme' or 'idealistic', its exponents were good-hearted and there could be no real enemy on the Left. After 1974 many lecturers were more worried about whether they themselves would still be in their posts in the next academic year than what any of their colleagues might be propagating. Furthermore, the main official inquiries into ITT showed almost complete indifference to what was actually being taught in courses. Even in books which claimed to make critical scrutinies of teacher education, such

---

53 Rosenthal, R. and Jackson, L. (1968). *Pygmalion in the Classroom*. New York: Holt, Rinehart & Winston.

as David Hencke's 1978 *Colleges in Crisis*, the specific content of ITT was largely ignored.[54] Confucianism, Flat-earthism or Scientology could have been significant influences on ITT for all the attention paid to what was taught or students told to read.

One important source of the strength of the New Left was educational publishing, with the Open University Press, Penguin Educational and Falmer Press early leaders in the field, soon to be followed by Routledge, which had earlier been the main publisher of serious liberal educational theoretical works, and Macmillan. One might suppose that by and large publishers are more interested in profit than ideology and conclude that those eager to publish New Left books, especially those deemed to be 'anti-sexist' and 'anti-racist', did so because such texts regularly appeared on compulsory reading lists in ITT. Yet on some occasions considerations of profit seem not to have been dominant. Penguin Educational, for example, declined to publish *The Rape of Reason: The Corruption of the Polytechnic of North London,* by Keith Jacka, Caroline Cox and John Marks, a penetrating exposure of abuses in higher education, including ITT. That book subsequently sold well when published by the small Churchill Press in 1975 and would have sold much better if Penguin Educational had published it. It seems to have been largely on the advice of Edward Boyle that Penguin Educational made its decision not to publish, perhaps in order not to antagonise the New Left to which by then the former Conservative minister had transferred his allegiance in matters educational.

Two campaigning groups deserve substantial credit, or blame, for the success of New Left educational ideas: the Forum of the Advancement of State Education, and the National Association for the Teaching of English (NATE). Two veteran communist figures of the Old Left, Brian Simon and Nanette Whitbread, edited *Forum,* which had a keen readership among ITT lecturers. Old Left Communists such as Harold and Nancy Rosen were also prominent in NATE, together with James Britton, Douglas Barnes and an able group of London teachers, several once at Walworth Comprehensive School, some of whom moved into teacher education in Bretton Hall and other North of England

---

54 Hencke, D. (1978). *Colleges in Crisis.* Harmondsworth: Penguin Education. Hencke was an education correspondent for the *Guardian* and *Times Higher Educational Supplement.*

colleges. Brian Simon and some other Old Left Marxists who gave considerable encouragement to New Left ideas and policies were later to criticise their effects, but seemed unwilling or unable to acknowledge their own responsibility for educational destructiveness.

With strong support from HMI for over twenty years, English teachers largely accepted the beliefs of the dominant groups in NATE, which were hostile to what was condemned as unnecessary and deadening formalism in language teaching. NATE favoured a sharp reduction in traditional language and literature studies, and promoted instead much greater time for students' discussions of their personal experiences. Many of the first generation of teacher educators, and teachers in general, who adopted this approach achieved success, since they themselves had solid grounding in the mainstream of English literature, as well as in grammar and spelling, and could provide sound guidance in language skills and guidance to wider reading, even though their courses were largely based on informal group activities. However, few of the students they taught were able in their turn to give such guidance when they became teachers. A vicious circle rapidly extended, because even those teacher educators of New English who realised that considerable numbers of their students were inadequate in basic language skills feared it would damage their self-esteem, and give heart to reactionaries, if the unpleasant truth were admitted.

The New Left and revolutionary defeatism

It is useful to consider the historical context in which neo-Marxist educational ideas in Britain and comparable countries arose. Domestically in Britain it seemed to many people in the late 1950s and 1960s that Harold Macmillan was right in supposing that they had 'never had it so good', although that was no reason for not wanting it to be much better. Real wages were higher, the working week shorter, and unemployment low, especially compared with the 1930s. In education Old Left campaigns for the end of the 11+ and creation of comprehensive secondary schools had largely succeeded, and the Conservatives were soon to raise the school-leaving age to 16, a long-planned development. Furthermore, student–teacher ratios had improved dramatically, despite the extension of the basic teacher training courses to three years, often capped by a fourth one. *Per capita* expenditure in primary and secondary education increased markedly under both Labour and Conservative governments, and numbers in higher education were swelling rapidly. An unending stream of audio-visual and other teaching aids were among the innovations heralded as stimulants to significant increases in educational standards.

Yet many on the Left felt acute disappointment that these major organisational changes had done little, if anything, to reduce gaps in average levels of educational attainment and qualification between different social groups. Some of the disappointment arose from irrational assumptions that children of, say, garbage collectors would achieve educational standards equal on average to those of children of, say, physicians, once the reforms they had advocated were implemented. There was a widespread reluctance within the New Left to examine the effects of changes it had promoted, such as the replacement of streaming or setting with mixed ability classes, even though in many instances these changes further depressed the average achievement of the groups the New Left hoped to help and increased educational differentials between those groups and others with higher 'cultural capital'. The gap in average educational standards between state and independent schools as shown, for example, by unadjusted A-Level results and relative proportions of Oxbridge entrants, increased during the 1970s after the disappearance in most areas of LEA grammar schools. Some social changes were outside the scope of schools to control, such as the rapid transformation of the ethnic composition of Britain, especially of large towns in England, after about 1958, but other changes were closely connected to the educational programme of the New Left, such as the reduced authority of teachers and the growth of a teenage youth culture significantly alienated from adult values. Yet the whole picture was not dismal and the sensible response to the failure of some earlier Left reforms would have been an honest and careful examination of what helped and what hindered improvements in educational standards among the mass of children, irrespective of comparisons with 'privileged' groups.

However, constructive responses were rare among the New Left, partly because of a marked weakening of belief in 'progress'. One important source of this crisis of confidence was the discredit accumulated by Communist regimes, especially after the Soviet invasion of Hungary in 1956 and Khrushchev's admissions of 1957 about the crimes of the Stalin era. Many non-Communist, indeed anti-Communist, western socialists were badly shaken, not only Communist Party members. Many on the New Left also began to fear that further rapid industrial and economic development would create environmental degradation and global catastrophe, rather than hasten socialism and higher living standards. The growing prestige of cultural relativism, as first popularised by the anthropologists Franz Boas and Margaret Mead with their claim that social values and judgements are purely internal to societies and that no society or sub-culture within one can be better than any other, also weakened the Old Left belief embodied in the title of Jacob Bronowski's widely read *The Ascent of Man*.

Much New Left educational thinking was, despite its revolutionary rhetoric, suffused with despair that much, if anything, of lasting value could be achieved in society as it was. The neo-Marxist view of the inutility of schools as agents of social change was well depicted by David Reynolds, then of University College, Cardiff, now of the University of Newcastle:

> school reform ... has been shown to be as worthwhile an enterprise as rearranging the furniture on S.S. Titanic. System reform on comprehensive lines has apparently failed to attain either a greater development of measurable academic talent or the fairer distribution of that talent or the increase in social class mixing that its proponents had hoped for. Specific innovations such as programmes of compensatory education, curriculum change, the employment of educational technology and even the development of more child-centred or progressive methods are remarkable for the lack of demonstrable effects that they have had upon any measurements of pupil outcome that have been utilised. Much research evidence also has accumulated which purports to show the impotence – not the importance – of schooling'.[55]

Reynolds added that 'studies such as *From Birth to Seven* that emanate from the National Children's Bureau' have 'merely served to strengthen the belief that schools can make little difference to the progress of their children.'

---

55 Reynolds, D. (1980). Review of M. Rutter, B. Maughan, P. Mortimore and J. Ouston with A. Smith (1979). *Fifteen Thousand Hours: Secondary Schools and their Effects on Children* in British Journal of Sociology of Education, 1 (2), p. 207.

Theoretical disputes among neo-Marxists during the 1970s and 1980s were often about two different kinds of educational defeatism. One kind held that schools merely reproduce existing class disparities and perpetuate capitalism. The French Marxist Louis Althusser described schools and universities as part of an ideological state apparatus which, as capitalism increases in maturity and cunning, becomes even more important for the maintenance of bourgeois power than the old repressive state apparatus of armed forces, police and prisons. In the United States Samuel Bowles and Herbert Gintis developed a 'correspondence theory', which held that 'different levels of education feed workers into different levels within the occupational structure and, correspondingly, tend toward an internal organisation compared to levels in the hierarchical division'.[56] Gintis claimed that 'capitalist' schools ensure that future workers 'are so conditioned that their preferences are endogenous to the production process'.[57] Bowles asserted that 'the children of managers and professionals are taught reliance within a broad set of constraints; the children of production workers are taught obedience'.[58] These propositions must surely have seemed absurd to every state school teacher by the 1970s, but they were the stock-in-trade of Open University courses and were widely influential in a large number of ITT and in-service courses. To succeed in their courses student teachers and experienced teachers alike had to compartmentalise their minds and ignore their own daily experiences.

The other kind of educational defeatism, in which British neo-Marxists were pioneers, urged that schools could and should be made into important sites of resistance to capitalism. Excitement at the prospect of revolution arising from schools rather than mines or factories was naturally stronger among teacher educators, who were safely out of classrooms, than among teachers who, irrespective of ideological stances, would be targets of abuse

---

56 Bowles, S. and Gintis, H. (1976). *Schooling in Capitalist America: Educational Reform and the Contradictions of Economic Life*. London: Routledge & Kegan Paul, p. 132.
57 Gintis, H. (1972). 'Towards a Political Economy of Education' in *Harvard Educational Review*, 42 (1), p. 271.
58 Bowles, S. (1965). 'Unequal Education and the Reproduction of the Social Division of Labour' in M. Carnoy (ed). *Schooling in Corporate Society: the Political Economy of Education in America*. New York: Mackay, p. 59.

and violence long before it became the turn of the police or military. Moreover, the most persuasive writer of the resistance faction, Paul Willis, exhibited little confidence that resistance by students to authority would get them or the wider reconstructionist forces very far.

Willis held that the importance of schools lay in 'social reproduction, or more exactly for their role in maintaining the conditions for continued material production in the capitalist mode', and in ensuring that the factories are filled on every Monday morning with 'workers displaying the necessary apparent gradations between mental and manual capacity and corresponding attitudes necessary to maintain, within broad limits, the present structure of class and production'.[59] In Willis' scheme, teachers help reproduce the capitalist order in one of three ways. Firstly, by feeding students with bourgeois ideology and its perverted version of knowledge, teachers may help shape them into efficient learners, and subsequently into efficient workers who make a specially high contribution to capitalist profits. This notion was expressed crudely by Rachel Sharp in a review of a book by Stephen Ball about a seaside secondary school:

> What indeed was going on at Beachside Comprehensive was the reproduction of labour power in a docile form to meet the economic, political and ideological requirements of a capitalist system based on exploitation ... This is the reality of the social processing that takes place at Beachside Comprehensive, the reality of selection for the wage labour system which characterises capitalist production and its profit-seeking dynamic ... This reality produces not only the underprivilege of working-class pupils in Beachside, but apartheid in South Africa, military dictatorships in much of the Third World, fascism in the 1930s, and poverty and human distress on a gigantic scale: in short, the reality of the world capitalist system.[60]

Secondly, one understands from Willis, teachers may, perhaps unconsciously, prepare young people for the soulless drudgery

---

59 Willis, P. (1977), op cit., pp. 171, 174.
60 Sharp, R. (1981). Review of Stephen Ball, *Beachside Comprehensive: a Case Study of Secondary Schooling* in *British Journal of Sociology of Education*, 2 (3), p. 282.

of mass production by boring them and thus rendering them listless and apathetic. Willis asserted

> The 'transition' from school to work, for instance, of working class kids who had really absorbed the rubric of self-development, satisfaction and interest in work, would be a terrifying battle. Armies of kids equipped with their 'self-concepts' would be fighting to enter the few meaningful jobs available, and masses of employers would be struggling to press them into meaningless work.

Thirdly, teachers may provoke working class boys to 'resist the established values and relationships of the established school.' Willis noted, all too truly, that 'many aspects of the lads' culture, for instance, are challenging and subversive and remain threatening'. Paul Corrigan argued that adolescent boys who disrupt classrooms and insult and humiliate teachers and other more law-abiding pupils should not be regarded as delinquents who pose a problem, but represent resistance to the power of the capitalist state, as symbolised in the school and its teachers, dismissed by him as middle class or bourgeois in so far as they try to earn their salaries by getting hostile youths to apply themselves to any forms of study.[61] Neo-Marxist feminists such as Lynn Davies of Birmingham University School of Education were quick to respond to the challenge and to assert that adolescent girls could resist teachers and disrupt schools at least as well as boys.[62]

However, Willis warned that 'this oppositional informal culture ... may well actually help to accomplish the wider social reproduction which the official policy has been trying to defeat or change'.[63] He maintained that 'in contradictory and unintended ways the counter-school culture actually achieves for education one of its main though misrecognised objectives – the direction of a proportion of working kids "voluntarily" to skilled, semi-skilled and unskilled manual work. Indeed, far from helping to cause the present "crisis" in education, the counter-school culture and the processes it sponsors has (sic) helped to prevent

---

61 Corrigan, P. (1979). *Schooling the Smash Street Kids.* London: Macmillan.
62 Davies, L. (1983) 'Gender, Resistance and Power' in S. Walker and L. Barton (eds). *Gender, Class and Education*. Lewes: Falmer Press.
63 Willis, P., 1977, p. 175.

a real crisis'.[64] Like the two earlier scenarios, the third one thus also proves advantageous to 'capitalism'. Willis' pessimism was shared by the influential historian of education Richard Johnson, who claimed, in an Open University textbook, that 'the most that can be hoped for is that they (such struggles) also help to develop struggles on other social sites'.[65] By 1986 Willis was suggesting that mass youth unemployment was 'an overwhelmingly working class and black working class phenomenon',[66] but he did not concede that his advice and that of other neo-Marxists had helped to bring this about. Nor did he question why the brown working class suffered less unemployment than the black.

No doubt most students in ITT who were lectured by neo-Marxist advocates of preparing in the classrooms for future resistance to predatory advanced capitalism took it all with more than a pinch of salt, but some future teachers were profoundly influenced by such messages. Some followed the logic of their beliefs by taking jobs in tough inner-city schools, which could, it seemed, speedily be converted into sites of resistance, since opposition to teachers was often rampant already. The most celebrated example of such a site of resistance was William Tyndale Primary School in North London.[67] Its head teacher and several of the staff were blamed by the Auld Report in 1976 for ruining the education of their pupils by failing to teach them very much of any value. Frank Musgrove noted that the head of William Tyndale 'had recently obtained his diploma in Primary Education (with a thesis on team teaching)' after which he had 'implemented a fair selection of the sociologically inspired cliches

---

64 ibid. p. 178.
65 Johnson, R. (1981). *Society, Education and the State*. Milton Keynes: Open University Press, p. 45.
66 Willis, P. (1986). 'Unemployment; the final inequality' in *British Journal of Sociology of Education,* 7 (2), p. 155.
67 William Tyndale was one of the first translators of the Bible into English, in the course of which he helped shape the modern English language. In 1536 Tyndale was first strangled and then burned as a heretic, at the orders of the Emperor Charles V in the Netherlands. His death is less celebrated than that of Sir Thomas More a year earlier, even though More was responsible for the deaths of several religious opponents and Tyndale was not. The shameful non-teaching at the William Tyndale Primary School may have the unfortunate effect that this great Englishman is commemorated even less in the future than hitherto.

in the repertoire of advanced diplomas for serving teachers'.[68] Musgrove concluded that 'the Tyndale affair was not a product of class conflict; it was the product of university-based in-service training'. The William Tyndale teachers were defended by Michael F. D. Young and Geoff Whitty, who in 1976 drew the lesson that

> As long as radical teachers remain isolated within their schools, and fail to develop links of solidarity with other teachers or work out ways of concretely identifying themselves with the broader working class movement for the transformation of society, they will lack the support and understanding of those groups upon whose power their capacity to resist the establishment will ultimately depend.[69]

Peter Musgrave, who had recently emigrated to an Australian chair in education, alleged that 'deviance imputed at the school was politicised by higher levels of the hierarchy',[70] although the Inner London Education Authority (ILEA) leadership had refrained from intervention for as long as possible and only did so finally after a litany of complaints from parents who were mainly Labour voters. Musgrave wrote this as part of a review of *Schools, Pupils and Deviance*, edited by Len Barton and Roland Meighan, in which he commended their interest in creating '*positive* deviance' in schools.[71]

Some neo-Marxists realised the absurdity of demanding ever more resources for education and more innovations, such as mainstreaming (the placing of children with various physical and cognitive defects in all-ability classes, in order to ensure there is no discrimination against them), if changes internal to education could have no significant results. Since 1945 the school leaving age had been raised from 14 to 16, teacher training from one year (Forces Educational Training Scheme) or two years to three or four years: how could this rate of expansion be kept up if *a priori* it was bound to be educationally ineffective this side of the revolution? There were therefore several attempts

---

68 Musgrove, F. (1979). *School and the Social Order.* Chichester: John Wiley, pp. 23–4; 193.
69 Whitty and Young (1976).
70 Musgrave, P. (1980). 'Where are We Going?' in *British Journal of Sociology of Education,* 1 (2), p. 223.
71 Italics as in Barton, L. and Meighan, R. (eds) (1979) *Schools, Pupils and Deviance*. Driffield: Nafferton Books, p. 6.

to define areas of 'limited autonomy' available to schools. The Centre for Contemporary Cultural Studies of Birmingham University conceded that 'in any specific historical situation industry's needs for labour are themselves extremely complex; they are not so much a question of the "requirements of the state" as the needs of different, co-existing capitals'.[72] Rosemary Deem of the Faculty of Educational Studies of the Open University agreed that, although 'the state in any capitalist country must try to meet the needs of capital and to provide conditions which are not inimical to the process of capitalist accumulation, this does not necessarily mean that there is a close fit between the functions of capital and those of the state, since capital is also heterogeneous, and what appeases one fraction will not do so for another'.[73] But, irrespective of whether the 'needs of capital' are simple or complex, and even if schools are allowed a modicum of autonomy, neo-Marxist theory was bound to have a depressing influence on student teachers.

Harold Silver's comment on Birmingham University's Centre for Cultural Studies *Unpopular Education: Schooling and Social Democracy in England since 1944* could have been applied to virtually every other New Left analysis:

> the massive, shaping presence of the capitalist state remained overwhelming in the argument – making the promised 'close and detailed description and analysis' superfluous. The dominant impression, as in Bowles and Gintis, was that whatever is done in the name of any liberal radical pressure is and must be wrong. Choice becomes illusory ... the outcome was to present reform as marginal to or a strengthening of the state ... Assertions to the contrary, and an awareness of the dilemma, did not prevent the analysis from massively using a model which ruled out any tangible negotiation or conflict that could change the position ... It became a case study in theory attempting to use, or to be, history, and in the ease with which history, theory and radical rhetoric can coexist without communicating.[74]

---

72 Education Group, Centre for Contemporary Cultural Studies (1981). *Unpopular Education: Schooling and Social Democracy in England since 1944.* London: Hutchinson, p. 21.
73 Deem, R. (1981). 'State Policy and Ideology in the Education of Women 1944–1980' in *British Journal of Sociology of Education*, 2 (2), p. 132.
74 Silver, H. (1983). *Education as History.* London: Methuen, pp. 251–2.

Neo-Marxists were assiduous in opposing claims that what schools do makes much difference to educational outcomes. One occasion for them to display their full range of argument was the publication in 1979 of the Rutter *et al. Fifteen Thousand Hours: Secondary Schools and their Effects on Children.*[75] Rutter and his colleagues compared the conduct and academic progress of secondary pupils in twelve comprehensive schools in the same South London borough and concluded that schools do make a difference, after every socio-cultural background variable has been taken into account. They found that the size, age or cost of the buildings and equipment, or staffing ratios, were not significant factors in the highly different educational outcomes in terms of examinations results, basic literacy and numeracy, and employability which they identified. What mattered most was the extent to which schools stressed academic work, planned syllabuses and prepare lessons carefully, paid individual attention to pupils, set homework regularly and marked it quickly with a lot of feedback, and encouraged extra-curricular activities and parental interest in school work.

Andy Hargreaves of the Faculty of Educational Studies at The Open University complained that *Fifteen Thousand Hours* failed to understand that gurus such as Bowles and Gintis had demonstrated convincingly that 'schools bolster up existing inequalities, rather than offsetting them'. Hargreaves attacked 'the measurement and specification' of variables in the study as 'hopelessly inadequate' and alleged that 'the cumulative effect of these methodological errors is a serious *under-estimation* of the influence of background characteristics on pupil outcomes and therefore a grave *over-estimation* of the effects of schooling per se' (emphasis as in original). Andy Hargreaves' final dismissal of *Fifteen Thousand Hours* was

> Its culmination in the concluding prescription that 'schools can do much to foster good behaviour and attainments, and that even in a disadvantaged area, schools can be a force for the good' is disturbing.[76]

---

75 Rutter, M., Maughan, B., Mortimore, P. and Ouston, J. with Smith, A. (1979). *Fifteen Thousand Hours: Secondary Schools and their Effects on Children.* London: Open Books.
76 Hargreaves, A. (1980). Review of *Fifteen Thousand Hours* in *British Journal of Sociology of Education,* 1 (2), pp. 212–16.

Tessa Blackstone, then a leading Labour figure in the ILEA and a prominent academic in Birkbeck College and later to become a peeress and a minister in the Blair Labour Government, noted that, although concerned parents, pupils and the public at large are well aware that individual teachers and the ethos of a particular school make a significant difference to standards of conduct and academic achievement, professional sociologists 'have been inclined to question if not discount such commonsense views'.[77] Unfortunately, it was the Andy Hargreaves brand of revolutionary defeatism that exerted intellectual hegemony over much of teacher education.

The situation in 1979

By the time the Conservatives came to office in 1979, the New Left had succeeded in undermining much of the tradition of encouraging civic virtue which had been an integral part of the instrumentalism of the old training colleges. New Left characterisation of liberal knowledge as a ploy to imbue victim groups with male, white, bourgeois ideology had become a new orthodoxy in many ITT courses. Some elements of the older child-centred traditions had been incorporated into the new dominant outlook but had been perverted in the process. The optimism of the Old Left had suffered even greater blows from the New Left than had beliefs of the teacher missionaries, the liberal educators and the older schools of child-centred thought.

Quite independently of any concerns about the quality of courses or any ideological disputes, morale among lecturers and students in ITT was at a very low point when the Conservatives returned to office in 1979. In 1960 the colleges contained 33,500 student teachers and in 1969 112,000. Numbers entering ITT courses increased from 20,468 in 1962, including PGCEs, to 43,436 in 1969. In 1969 the Association of Teachers in Colleges and Departments of Education (ATCDE) nonetheless passed a conference resolution that the government should expand the colleges to 220,000 students, including, however, a few who might not intend to teach. By 1972, when there were 117,000 students in the colleges, the DES warned that, in order to prevent future teacher unemployment and to save resources, the

---

77 Blackstone, T. (1980). Review of *Fifteen Thousand Hours* in *British Journal of Sociology of Education,* 1 (2), p. 216.

colleges' capacity should fall to 59,000 in 1981. Its Permanent Secretary Hugh Harding suggested 42,000 places would be more than adequate. In 1975 the DES reduced the estimated need for college places in 1981 to 58,500 and the entry number to under 13,000. Just one year later in 1976 a further fall in the birth rate led the DES to cut the 1981 projected figure to 45,000 places.

By 1977 20,000 newly qualified teachers were unable to find teaching posts. The rapid fall in numbers in ITT helped to accelerate moves to abolish single-purpose colleges of education, either by making them part of polytechnics and other colleges of higher education, all later to be retitled universities, or ending them entirely. By 1976 only 30,000 students remained in 30 single-purpose colleges surviving from over 160 a decade earlier. Most former college lecturers who become university academics seemed initially pleased with their change in status, but some soon felt considerable anxiety about new challenges and possible redundancy. Those actually displaced, naturally enough, felt no pleasure at all, other than in thinking about what to do with their redundancy packages.

There were many rational explanations for errors in calculation by the DES and all others concerned for forecasting the needs of the schools: in the post-war years early motherhood was much more popular with young women than before and during the war, but a reaction set in during the 1960s, so that from a peak of 870,000 children born in England and Wales in 1964 the number fell to 602,000 in 1975. The number of new babies born fell in more or less the same proportions that more women teachers stayed in the classrooms instead of retiring. In addition, returning to teaching after their children reached their teens became much more popular with women during the late 1960s, a trend strengthened by the big pay increase awarded to teachers in 1974 by the Houghton Committee. Since the Houghton Committee did not differentiate between fields of teacher shortage and teacher surplus, the education unions still felt able to use shortages of mathematics and physics teachers in secondary schools to prop up the number of places for primary teachers in the colleges, but with little success, as the oil crisis of 1974 led to a run on sterling and calls for reduced public expenditure all round. The colleges themselves were often caught in a difficult position: they were expected to mount courses with adequate numbers to justify the cost, but it was hard to attract entrants into shortage subjects – that is why the schools were short of them! On the other hand, it was easy to enrol students for primary teaching and for most arts and humanities subjects in secondary schools, naturally the areas in which there were very few vacancies.

It is sometimes claimed that central government control is necessary to ensure that there is a sufficiency, but not a huge surplus, of the types of teacher needed for different types of school. Yet it is almost impossible to conceive that grosser errors in forecasting could have taken place since 1945 if independent providers had been operating in market conditions. Nor has close government control over numbers entering ITT been justified by results in other countries. In New Zealand, for example, instead of ensuring regularity of supply, central planning created alternating periods of teacher shortage and surplus.[78] It would be much preferable if a voucher system were introduced whereby providers could recruit qualified entrants irrespective of forecasts about future teacher demand and supply. Any information, or indeed informed guesswork, possessed by the government should, of course, be made available to all interested in teaching as a career, but the number of places in teacher education should be left to market forces. Provided that no entrants are led to believe that they are certain of future employment as teachers, suitable applicants should not be excluded from ITT, any more than from arts, science or any other courses, within the overall finance available for tertiary education as a whole. Withholding part of funding until entrants into ITT have been appointed to a teaching post, perhaps until they have completed a given minimum of service, would help to ensure that HEIs, and schools in SCITT schemes were realistic in the numbers they sought to recruit and ambitious about the standards they sought to achieve.

The educational unions rarely expressed any satisfaction in any situation: during periods of rapid expansion they complained of overcrowding and inadequate resources, periods of rapid contraction raised fears of redundancies and staff demoralisation, while the few stable years were castigated as evidence of stagnation. Yet, then as now, they utterly condemned opening ITT to market forces. In 1978 David Hencke

---

78 See Partington, 1997, ch. 3.

blamed the current Labour ministers as well as their Conservative predecessors:

> Obviously no group of ministers or civil servants has consciously planned such a dramatic growth and decline within a mere sixteen years. But they did authorise the spending of millions of pounds on modernising and rebuilding ancient colleges during the wave of expansion, only to agree later to an escalating closure programme which left buildings and equipment under-used and whole campuses to be sold on the open market.[79]

Hencke portrayed unfavourably nearly all education ministers during the five-year period on which he concentrated. These were four Secretaries of State: Margaret Thatcher, Reg Prentice, Fred Willey and Shirley Williams; and four Ministers of State responsible for higher education: Norman St John-Stevas, Gerry Fowler, Lord Crowther-Hunt and Gordon Oakes. Margaret Thatcher and Lord Crowther-Hunt emerge from his pages as perhaps a cut above the others, but all lacked vision. Hencke's strongest dislike was for permanent officials at the DES, such as Hugh Harding and Sir Toby Weaver. Yet, in spite of his strictures, his call was for more power at the centre, exercised wisely, of course.

It certainly could not be alleged that any weaknesses in teacher education in the late 1970s resulted from policies urged by politicians of either major party, although they may be accused of neglect in allowing follies to flourish. Large numbers of parliamentarians, and for that matter councillors in local government, of all political shades assumed that, although many of the educational ideas presented to them seemed on the face of it decidedly strange, they must make some sense since so many professional educationists held them. The politicians and councillors had more excuse perhaps than the courtiers who praised the Emperor's new clothes, since there were only two tailors at that court, whereas a regular army of educational academics and professional spokespersons extolled their wares. Uncritical acceptance of what educationalists told them was common among Conservatives as well as others. As Christopher Chataway, who served as Parliamentary Secretary to the Ministry

---

79 Hencke, 1978, p. 11.

of Education under Sir Edward Boyle, a man highly impressed by the tailors of education, put it, 'Relatively few Conservative MPs then took much interest in education, and, since nearly all of them had been to private schools themselves, most knew very little about the maintained system'.[80]

What the educationists claimed seemed odd, but then Einstein's theories and much besides seemed strange to lay persons, but were apparently well supported. Sir Edward, by then Vice-Chancellor of the University of Leeds, gave a hostile reception to the Black Papers, whose arguments anticipated many of the post-1978 Conservative reforms in education,[81] as did Lord [Rab] Butler and most Conservative leaders who made any public comment. The power of the media helped to silence criticism of progressive educational orthodoxy. In particular, the Education Correspondents Group formed in the 1960s was active in deriding doubters.[82] Angus Maude was one of the few politicians before 1979 to challenge the New Left hegemony in public, although Rhodes Boyson was a prominent critic both before and after entering Parliament.

As Secretary of State for Education and Science, Margaret Thatcher was typical of most Conservative members in her lack of detailed recent knowledge of government schools, let alone teacher education. In retrospect she decided that the Plowden Committee, appointed by Sir Edward Boyle, had 'sent the primary schools in the wrong direction' when it 'leaned strongly in favour of teaching in small groups and even one-to-one, rather than classes', but she 'had no strong views on the matter' when she 'arrived at the DES'. Her 'doubts only started to surface' when she 'visited schools and found that in reality individual children were often not being taught in a group, let alone in a class, but were left to their own – not necessarily very useful –

---

80 In Gould, A. (ed) (1991). *Edward Boyle: His Life by his Friends*. London: Macmillan.
81 One example was the call in Black Paper Two by Mrs D. M. Pinn, head teacher of Henrietta Barnett Primary School in North London that lecturers in colleges and departments of education should remain in post for only five years before returning to a school for at least a year.
82 The group included Tudor David of *Education*, Roy Nash of the *Daily Mail*, Peter Newell and Stuart Maclure of the *Times Educational Supplement*, Nicholas Bagnall of the *Sunday Telegraph*, Anne Corbett of *New Society*, Brian Macarthur of *The Times*, Shirley Toulson of *The Teacher*, and Bruce Kemble of the *Daily Express*.

devices'.[83] She became more and more convinced that 'increases in public spending had not by and large led to higher standards' and that 'too many teachers were less competent and more ideological than their predecessors'. She 'distrusted the new "child-centred" teaching techniques, the emphasis on imaginative engagement rather than learning facts' and 'knew from parents, employers and pupils themselves that too many people left school without a basic knowledge of reading, writing and arithmetic'.[84]

Margaret Thatcher noted that 'years after many people in the Labour Party had begun to have their doubts, the educationists retained a sense of mission'.[85] The educationists she had in mind included her own civil servants – she held that 'the ethos of the DES was self-righteously socialist' – and most teacher educators. Nevertheless, at the DES Margaret Thatcher had little influence on the content of teacher education. She admitted later, with reference to the James Committee she appointed, 'in effect, I got nowhere in my attempts to get the curriculum of teacher training institutions discussed within the planned inquiry. It was still taboo for politicians to get involved in such matters. Fifteen years later the situation had not materially improved'.[86]

The most senior politician to draw public attention to the nakedness of some much-lauded educational institutions was not a Conservative, but James Callaghan in his 1976 Ruskin College speech. Callaghan's attack on the combination of low educational standards with high public spending on education originated in his feeling that his grandchildren were receiving an inferior primary education to that his children had gained in far larger classes under teachers who had received a shorter period of teacher training. Although acknowledging that his Ruskin speech represented worries held 'beyond' the Conservative Party, Martyn Hammersley of the School of Education, Open University, still maintained in 1996 that Callaghan's concern was that teacher educators were advocating 'progressivist ideology'.[87] But Callaghan was not so much interested in whether

---

83 Thatcher, M. (1995). *The Path to Power*, London: HarperCollins, pp. 184–5.
84 Thatcher, M. (1993). *The Downing Street Years.* London: HarperCollins, p. 590.
85 Thatcher, 1995, p. 166.
86 Thatcher, 1995, p. 177.
87 Hammersley, M. (1996). 'Post Mortem or Post Modern? some Reflections on British Sociology of Education' in *British Journal of Educational Studies*, 44 (4), p. 397.

teaching methods were progressivist or traditional as in whether they worked, especially for working-class children. In Australia it was Australian Labor Party (ALP) governments which first gave effect after 1983 to public concern about educational standards in ways often similar to those adopted in Britain by the Conservatives. A left-wing Australian trade unionist, Lawrie Carmichael, headed one of the three influential reports (Mayer, Finn and Carmichael) which sought to replace school-based monitoring of student achievement, distrusted widely by the late 1980s, with industrial systems used in apprenticeship. However, despite Callaghan's expression of concern, it was only with the accession to power of Margaret Thatcher that serious reforms to teacher education in Britain were undertaken.

Many anti-government resolutions were passed by committees and conferences of teacher education organisations between 1974 and 1979, but the Labour Party in office did not excite the ferocious denunciations that the Conservatives would have faced had they been in government then. Within a short time UCET and wellnigh the whole education industry were looking back to the pre-1979 years as if to a golden age, calm before the storms released by New Right ideologies during the Thatcher regime. Margaret Wilkin has suggested that the 1970s saw increased emphasis on 'competence', more time relatively on teaching practice and a more applied approach to educational theory, so that 'by the time the Conservative government came to power in 1979, the curriculum of teacher training had begun to exhibit what can now be seen to be sub-Thatcherite tendencies; and what is more this had come about through the action of the profession'.[88] This may have been the case in some institutions, but overall the dominance of New Left thinking was even greater in ITT at the end of the 1970s than at their beginning. Geoff Whitty of Goldsmith's College, University of London, recalled in 1992 that when he first joined a university department of education in 1981

> courses had no explicit statements of purpose nor was there any discussion among staff about how different parts of the course related to one another let alone to an overall purpose. I was told

---

[88] Wilkin, M. (1995). 'Overview' of her *Initial Teacher Training: The Dialogue of Ideology and Culture* presented to the Australian Teacher Education Association Conference, Sydney, p. 7.

in all seriousness by my head of department that I could not ask for details of what was being taught elsewhere on a course to which I contributed, since that would be to abuse my colleagues' academic freedom. What was taught was essentially left to the discretion of individual academics and, to my knowledge, no explicit monitoring and evaluation ever took place.[89]

But Whitty did not go on to congratulate the Conservatives in helping his hapless colleagues to achieve at least a slightly clearer sense of professional purpose.

In 1979 Frank Musgrove summed up the theoretical state of the sociology of education under neo-Marxist hegemony as follows

... one wonders at the intellectual shoddiness of it all, the spectacle of modest talents on the make. It has been a tawdry, over-hasty, but curiously bombastic exercise as reviewed in this book, pretentious and arrogant, often with careless, incompetent or none too scrupulous treatment of evidence either through cowardice in the face of fashion or perhaps unawareness that truth matters.[90]

Stephen Ball of the Centre for Educational Studies, King's College, London, admitted in 1995 that sociology of education, his own discipline, had 'always been politically committed' and 'particular policy solutions, based upon the outcomes of empirical research, were pursued, particularly in relation to Labour Party policy-making'.[91] Ball recalled that until the early 1970s these sociologists were highly optimistic that their assaults on traditional academic structures would have wondrous results, but he admitted that 'this dual optimism (that attached to the welfare state and that embedded in the practices and discourses of the discipline itself) did not last' and that 'in the 1970s the academic discourse of programmatic optimism was to be dramatically and decisively replaced by one of radical pessimism ... the reproduction of unequal social relations were

---

89 Whitty, G. (1992). Quality Control in Teacher Education' in *British Journal of Educational Studies,* XXXX (1), p. 38.
90 Musgrove, 1979, p. 193.
91 Ball, S. J. (1995). 'Intellectuals or Technicians? The Urgent Role of Theory in Educational Studies' in *British Journal of Educational Studies*, XXXXIII (3), p. 257.

discovered to be lurking stubbornly in every classroom nook and cranny ...'.[92]

Eric Hoyle and Peter John of the University of Bristol School of Education 'do not accept the charge that teacher training between 1964 and 1976 caused a decline in teaching skills from those achieved in some prelapsarian period. Nor do we deny it. The reformers have no hard evidence as to whether or not such a decline occurred. Neither have we'.[93] Hoyle and John did not ask themselves why there was little or no evidence, hard or soft, to enable any informed judgement to be made about so expensive and important an undertaking, and blithely dismissed all charges as 'mainly anecdotal' imputations against those they jocosely term 'the usual suspects'. Hoyle wrote some excellent work, notably his valuable accounts of different types of professionalism, during his Bristol professorship. Perhaps he was too busy to notice that several of his colleagues were prime candidates for inclusion in the indictment drawn up by Frank Musgrove.

In addition to concerns of recent origin about neo-Marxist hegemony over teacher education achieved during the 1970s, were older misgivings about the relevance to schools of educational theories as a whole. The criticism made by Anthony Hartnett of Philip Robinson's *Perspectives on the Sociology of Education: an Introduction*, Beverley Shaw's *Educational Practice* and Roland Meighan's *A Sociology of Educating*, all published in 1981, was accepted by many both within and outside the ranks of professional educators as true of the disciplines of education as a whole:

> Different as these books are in their tone and in the ways that they present their material, none offers any *argument* as to why teachers and other professionals in the area of educational practice and policy should be interested in the books or should believe that they have any relevance to their work (emphasis as in original).[94]

Hartnett himself believed, of course, that educational disciplines were, and could be shown to be, highly relevant to the needs of

---

92 Ball, 1995, p. 258.
93 Hoyle and John, 1998, pp, 76; 69.
94 Hartnett, A. (1983). 'The Sociology of Education and the Education of Teachers: Arguments for a Reconsideration of the Relationship' in *British Journal of Sociology of Education,* 4 (1), p. 87.

schools, but he was unconvinced that 'the move from being able to pack all sociologists of education into a telephone box (in the good old days) to now needing the Albert Hall is to be put down to the quality of sociological thought and its rapid recognition in non-sociological circles'.[95] It was hardly surprising that many Conservative politicians should by 1979 have become highly sceptical of the quality of much of the thinking displayed in ITT.

---

95 Hartnett, 1983, p. 92.

3 | The Conservative Reforms

In respect of education as a whole Conservative governments after 1979 had to some extent to choose between two strategies which had opposite implications for central control. In ideal conditions most Conservatives would have preferred to reduce central control and to free up the education system by giving more choice to parents and more independence to schools. Some important steps in that direction were taken, such as the Parents' Charter and Assisted Places Scheme of 1980 which extended choice for pupils of high academic ability. Later moves included the 1988 Education Reform Act's encouragement to open enrolment by allowing popular schools to expand to their full physical capacity, the Local Management of Schools (LMS) Initiative, which gave managers and governors much more extensive powers than in the past, and the creation of grant-maintained schools, free completely from LEA control and directly funded from the DES. City technology colleges also extended choice.

On the other hand extensions of parental choice and greater freedom of action for schools seemed to many Conservatives to be unable, at least for an unduly lengthy period, to end or amend schools of the William Tyndale type. By 1979 Margaret Thatcher herself favoured a national curriculum of some sort, if only because 'it was disruptive if children who moved from a school in one area to a school elsewhere found themselves confronted with a course of work different in almost all respects from that to which they had become accustomed' and she supported too 'a nationally recognised and reliably monitored system of testing at various stages of the child's school career to know what was going right and wrong and take remedial action if necessary'. Equally, however, she 'never believed' that 'the state should try to regiment every detail of what happened in schools', as she took to be the case in France.[96] Her experience

---

96 Thatcher, 1993, p. 591.

at the DES led her to 'the conclusion that there had to be some consistency in the curriculum, at least in the core subjects', but she also asserted, 'What I never believed, though, was that the state should try to regiment every detail of what happened in schools'. Yet, as she was quick to realise, 'even the strictly limited objectives I set for the national curriculum were immediately seen by the vested interests in education as an opportunity to impose their own agenda'.[97] Whether one or more than one friend of those vested interests deliberately guided the 1987 Task Group on Assessment and Testing to 'regiment every detail', perhaps with the intention of stirring up as much teacher opposition as possible, or whether Kenneth Baker achieved this effect without any activity by *agents provocateurs* remains uncertain, but the final result was much as Margaret Thatcher had feared. In the event bottom-up decentralising policies which gave parents and schools greater freedom from bureaucratic control were accompanied by top-down measures which gave the central bureaucracy new and greater powers than ever before.

The key top-down reforms were the introduction of a detailed 10 level, 4 key stage National Curriculum, backed by national testing at ages 7, 11, 14 and 16, and compulsory league tables, with the Education Reform Act (1988) the most important legislation. OFSTED was established to carry out regular inspections to assess each school's management, efficiency and teaching methods. OFSTED was supported by the Schools' Curriculum and Assessment Authority (SCAA), which was the result of a merger in 1994 between the National Curriculum Council (NCC) and the Schools Examinations and Assessment Committee (SEAC) and had the responsibility for advising schools on what should be taught and how their teaching should be assessed. Overall, the result was greater central control of school curricula than at any previous time during the twentieth century.

Several minor revisions and one major one were made in subsequent years, many in response to constructive criticisms by head teachers and class teachers. The NUT and other teacher unions, together with many teacher educators, complained about frequent changes, just as they would have complained about intransigence and refusal to listen to complaints

---

97 Thatcher, 1993, pp. 590–1.

and suggestions had no changes been made, or only a few. Comparably, if specification of curriculum and subsequent inspection of standards had been confined to 'basics', the educational unions would have regarded that as proof that the Conservatives had no interest in wider aspects of knowledge and culture, but extensive and elaborate specification and testing was held by them to prove that the Conservatives were determined to regulate the entire curriculum and to deprive teachers of any independence whatsoever. Margaret Thatcher had experience of this in her time at the DES. She recalled being accused by a delegation from the NUT that she had 'resigned responsibility for giving shape to education' by failing to act as the union wished, but she did not think the NUT would have liked the shape she would have given it.[98] But the fact that some interest groups may oppose a government, irrespective of the merits of its policies, does not entail that all those policies are right and all the criticisms mistaken. The top-down reforms were an understandable reaction against the excesses over a quarter of a century of the New Left, but not all reactions against follies are themselves wise.

The whole concept of a National Curriculum for schools was driven by a belief that many pupils lacked knowledge they ought to possess. Similarly the National Curriculum for ITT was driven by a justified conviction that many teachers lacked knowledge they ought to have. In the face of the growing evidence of teacher inadequacy, HMI and others expressed increasing doubts about the past effectiveness of teacher education and called in particular for a major increase in specialist subject teaching.[99] Support for this view was provided from within teacher education. David Hargreaves wrote in 1994 that 'primary teachers' relative lack of knowledge about and expertise in, teaching subjects such as physical science, history and geography have been ruthlessly exposed by the National Curriculum and this is openly acknowledged'.[100]

---

98 Thatcher, 1995, p. 169.
99 See Alexander, R., Rose, J. and Woodhead, C. (1992). *Curriculum Organisation and Classroom Practice in Primary Schools*. London: Department of Education and Science.
100 Hargreaves D. H. (1994). 'The New Professionalism: The Synthesis of Professional and Institutional Development' in *Teaching and Teacher Education*, 10 (4) p. 426.

In their 1993 *Learning to Teach* Neville Bennett and Clive Carre reported research into the subject expertise of 59 graduates engaged in a one-year course in primary teacher education in the University of Exeter. Their research exposed the weak knowledge basis of these intending teachers. In science, for example, 'many did not have a bank of concepts from which they could confidently apply their knowledge to make sense of everyday phenomena'.[101] Even at the end of their PGCE course the group was lower on average in science than those of the top 20 per cent of 11 year olds. On one question the Music and Early Years graduates enrolled in the Exeter PGCE were weaker than average 11 year olds. Direct comparison was possible because the test items were those devised for 11 year olds by the Assessment of Performance Unit in the DES. Only 6 out of 10 graduate students got the right answer to: 'What is 18 as a percentage of 120?', the range of answers extending from 3 per cent to 666 per cent. By the end of their PGCE, 'when faced with diagnosing a child's error to a non-routine problem, there was very little change – if anything the student teachers got worse'.[102]

In teacher education the strategic issue for the government was whether to free up the system by opening up entry into teaching in the hope that head teachers, managers and governors would choose applicants whose training, or avoidance of it, best suited their needs, or to take decisive steps to make ITT in existing institutions more efficient. Both approaches were employed, but 'top-down' reforms had precedence. They were based on a conviction that candidates for the award of Qualified Teacher Status (QTS), whatever may have been their mode of professional training, must be able to demonstrate attainment of professional standards relevant to their area of teaching. Whereas the first group of policies reduced central controls, the second group increased them. It was almost inevitable that conflicts would arise between arguments that suitable graduates, or in the case of 'Mums' Army' suitable persons with sufficient experience with children, should be encouraged to enter teaching with little or no formal training, and claims that ITT in established institutions must be much more strictly defined and monitored.

---

101 Carre, C. in Bennett, N. and Carre, C. (1993). *Learning to Teach*. London: Routledge, p. 25.
102 Bennett and Carre, 1993, p. 47.

The 1983 DES publication *Teaching Quality* claimed that teacher education was often inefficient and responsible for mismatches between what teachers had been prepared to do and what they were actually required to do in schools. It argued that 'Initial teacher training courses are not always sufficiently closely geared to the needs of our schools; and some teachers are asked to undertake teaching programmes in parts of the curriculum for which the specialist elements of their education and training have not prepared them'.[103] This was true enough, though not always the fault of teacher education. Given that there were 'shortage' subjects, such as mathematics, and 'surplus' subjects such as history, it is hardly surprising that, for example, some secondary heads put pressure on history graduates on their staff who had been mathematically competent themselves at school to teach junior maths classes. Some secondary heads deliberately chose primary trained young teachers to deal with pupils with learning difficulties.

Early steps aimed at making ITT more efficient were the establishment in 1984 for a period of three years (later extended to five years) of the first Council for the Accreditation of Teacher Education (CATE 1), which was to advise the Secretary of State on whether courses in ITT should be approved, and the requirements in DES Circular 3/84 that teacher educators should have 'recent and relevant' experience in the sort of classroom in which their student teachers were to teach, and that teachers should play a more central part in teacher education, including selection of applicants for courses. CATE replaced the Schools Council which, since 1964, had brought the main allies in the education industry (unions, ITT providers, LEAs, DES and HMI) together harmoniously, so that destructive innovations could be introduced with virtually no opposition.

The first major 'bottom-up' reform was the introduction in 1989 of the Licensed Teacher Scheme, which was mainly used to recruit applicants who were of mature age (over 24), had gained at least C grade in GCSE in English and mathematics and had at least two years higher education in shortage subjects, but who lacked standard qualifications for qualified teacher status. The Articled Teacher Scheme, which ran from 1989 to

---

103 DES (1983). *Teaching Quality*. London: HMSO, p. 2.

1994, enabled graduates to enter into a two-year programme of school-based induction into teaching, with 80 per cent of the time spent in schools. Entrants received a bursary of £14,000 a year, a much higher amount than the then maximum grant of £2,265 a year for PGCE students, plus up to another £2,000 in extreme shortage subjects. It was found that the 80 per cent spent in schools under the Articled Scheme was too much and the proportion was lowered to 66 per cent by Kenneth Clarke. In 1996 a Graduate Teacher Scheme was introduced, comparable to the Licensed Teacher Scheme, except that graduates could be awarded QTS after one term of teaching deemed of a satisfactory standard.

The pace of change quickened in 1992 when the Department for Education (DfE) required that newly qualified teachers must demonstrate a specified set of 'competences', later altered to 'standards', which were to be regarded as constituting 'the heart of the criteria' for the acceptability of teacher education courses. The full policy was based on the application to teacher education of the principles on which the National Curriculum for schools had been gradually worked out over the previous years. This linkage is a double one, since the introduction of the National Curriculum into the schools had the effect of drawing attention much more sharply than in the past to incompetence, especially in lack of subject knowledge, displayed by many teachers, including many with extensive experience.

Circular 9/92 introduced a new type of partnership between schools and teacher education institutions, with the schools enjoying far wider powers and responsibilities than in the past. The DfE required that in future training of primary teachers schools 'should play a much larger and more influential role in course design and delivery'. In respect of secondary schools 9/92 stipulated

> The Government expects that partner schools and HEIs [Higher Educational Institutions] will exercise a joint responsibility for the planning and management of courses and the selection, training and assessment of students. The balance of responsibilities will vary. Schools will have a leading responsibility for training students to teach their specialist subjects, to assess pupils and to manage classes, and for supervising students and assessing their competence in these respects. HEIs will be responsible for ensuring that courses meet the requirements for academic validation, presenting

courses for accreditation, awarding qualifications to qualified students and arranging student placements in more than one school.[104]

This circular set out requirements for the training of secondary phase teachers, including

> demonstration of subject knowledge with particular reference to the relevant sections of the National Curriculum;
>
> ability to apply subject knowledge through coherent lesson plans and appropriate teaching strategies;
>
> competent class management;
>
> competent assessment and recording of pupils' progress; and
>
> capacity for further professional development.

Following on an HMI Report which claimed that about one third of lessons its inspectors observed being taught by newly qualified teachers were unsatisfactory, Circular 14/93 was issued by the DES with the aim of ensuring that 'teachers are better fitted to play their central role in implementing new policies and achieving the higher standards which are the aim of the Government's reforms'.[105] 14/93, which marked a substantial increase in the effective power exercised over ITT providers by the central government, established new criteria to be met by all providers of primary school ITT, including a higher proportion of time in HEIs to be spent on mathematics, science and English, a minimum of 150 hours of 'directed time' in English, mathematics and science being stipulated. Primary postgraduate courses were lengthened from 36 to 38 weeks. Entry requirements were to include a C grade in a science subject as well as in English and mathematics. More student time to be spent on teaching practice, which was to be controlled by a partnership between schools and HEI, but with the former in the dominant role. ITT courses were to be planned by HEIs in partnership with schools. All providers of ITT were to establish and maintain profiles of competencies 'which will be useful for

---

104 DES Circular 9/92, para. 14.
105 DES (1993). Circular 14/93: *The Government's Proposals for the Reform of Initial Teacher Education,* p. 1.

intending employers and will form a basis for further professional development through induction and in-service training'.[106] Groups of schools wishing to develop their own ITT independently of HEIs were invited to apply for funding – the origin of SCITT.

If primary schools were to undertake these tasks more effectively than 14/93 implied HEIs had done in the past, more subject expertise would be needed than many had available. The suggestion that it would be 'helpful to identify co-ordinators who can assist and train other staff' was something of an understatement. It would not be easy to ensure that each primary school had specialist teachers with 'specific subject strengths' who could train their colleagues to reach competence at Key Stage Two in the relevant subject or even to provide 'timetabled subject teaching' in the upper primary classes before pupils move on to secondary school.[107] If large numbers of primary teachers with the knowledge and skill to undertake these duties had been already available, there would have been much less need for educational reform.

The first draft of 14/93 contained a proposal for a faster mode of entry into nursery and infant teaching for persons with 'considerable previous experience of working with young children (such as nursery nurses who have worked for some time in schools) with the necessary qualifications for entry to higher education'.[108] An outcry among teacher unions and HEIs against dilution of the teaching profession by a 'Mums' Army' led to a modification of this proposal. In the final 14/93 it was proposed that classroom assistants should be trained and certified in order to help with actual teaching in the classroom, under the supervision of a teacher with full QTS. The assistants would undertake 'a variety of tasks including preparing materials, working with small groups of children under supervision, and listening to children reading'.[109] This modified version received almost equal denunciation as the original proposal.

The pace of ITT reform quickened again with the establishment of the TTA and support for SCITT. The TTA replaced CATE in September 1994 under the 1994 Education Act. The

---

106 14/93, p. 7.
107 14/93, p. 6.
108 Draft 14/93, p. 12.
109 14/93, p. 11.

TTA, like OFSTED and SCAA, is directly answerable to the Secretary of State, who has the power to nominate all its members, although these must be chosen from both outside and within the ranks of professional educators. The TTA was given responsibility for recruitment and staffing, the content and practice of teaching, and funding; it was 'to secure a diversity of high quality and cost-effective initial training which ensures that new teachers have the knowledge, understanding and skills to teach pupils effectively', and in ways which rewarded 'cost-effectiveness and diversity'.[110] The TTA, not HEIs, now determines what constitutes 'high quality teaching and teacher education' and what are the 'key features of effective classroom and training practice'.

The TTA soon went beyond CATE's profiles of initial teacher competency to develop a full-scale National Curriculum for ITT. The TTA made fulfilment of QTS standards, which it controlled, central to entry into teaching, rather than achievement of awards by HEIs such as the BEd or PGCE. It would be up to HEIs to ensure that their awards satisfied QTS requirements, since their own endorsement of their students' competencies would no longer suffice. The University of Lancaster was the first institution whose awards were refused QTS by the TTA. A major feature of the QTS standards required by the TTA is that all of the hundred or so must be achieved and demonstrated in their entirety at the end of the training period before QTS status may be granted. No principle of compensation operates for any weaknesses or failures. Within a relatively short time TTA radically changed the nature of the ITT partnerships between schools and HEIs and the balance of the courses conducted within the HEIs.

The Scottish Office Education Department (SOED) issued comparable guidelines, which, as Cameron-Jones and O'Hara noted, were 'in effect requirements', for competences to be demonstrated by 'the new Scottish teacher'.[111] The SOED also proposed that teaching skills in the areas of 'class management and curriculum' are best developed in the schools, not in tertiary institutions. However, the Scottish statement offered a broader

---

110 TTA Corporate Plan, 1996, pp 12; 10.
111 Cameron-Jones, M. and O'Hara, P. (1995). 'Students' Expectations of Influence on their Competence in Initial Teacher Education' in *Studies in Higher Education*, 20 (3), p. 330.

definition of 'professional competences' than any provided by the Department for Education for England and Wales, stipulating that these 'should be taken to refer to knowledge, understanding, critical thinking and positive attitudes, as well as to practical skills'. Basically the same approach was also taken by the Department of Education for Northern Ireland.

Once embarked on 'top-down' centralist controls in ITT, it was almost inevitable that the TTA should move on to consider in-service training for serving teachers, including head teachers. By 1996 a Head Teachers' Professional Qualification had been developed as a prerequisite for future promotions. There can be no doubt that even highly experienced teachers may be inadequately prepared to undertake some duties of headship, as I was when appointed Head of Bungay Modern School in 1968 by the then East Suffolk County Council. Whether Governors and Managers should be limited to appointing to headships only applicants who have undergone a pre-headship course, or for that matter ITT, is, however, a very different proposition.

SCITT schemes enabled consortia of schools to offer postgraduate teacher training to graduates who may thereby obtain QTS without securing an academic award of an HEI. These consortia receive direct funding for teacher education but may then buy support services from HEIs, instead of HEIs themselves directly receiving a grant for each student and then negotiating with schools for teaching practice placements. Funding for 1993–94 courses was £4,000 per student, the average for HEI providers, but in addition consortia could reclaim up to £15,000 in start-up costs.

By the time the Conservatives lost office in 1997 only a few schools had opted for SCITT. The first results should encourage more schools to take part but they fail to persuade that SCITT should become the only or the main form of ITT. Many students believe that what they experience in their practice school is far more relevant and important to their professional development than anything that goes on outside it. That sentiment is not irrational or indefensible, but teachers will in the normal course of events engage in that type of experience year in and year out, whereas other components of ITT do not recur in ordinary professional life. Haberman's argument that beginning teachers should experience as much as possible as soon as possible of conditions likely to be met in difficult classrooms has something in it, but there are also legitimate fears about putting beginners in at the deep end. SCITT cannot compete with HEI-based ITT in availability of expert knowledge about educational ideas and teaching methods which flourish beyond the bounds of the practice school and the group to which it may belong. In addition, library facilities and course materials are almost bound to be inferior, although the gap may well be rapidly reduced as SCITT continues. However, a major concern must be that the tendency to regard one way of teaching as the only sensible one is often especially strong when ITT takes place entirely within a single school. This is not to deny that there is also a danger that some student teachers in HEI-based ITT may be led by their lecturers to feel an unjustified superiority to the practices of schools to which they are attached.

In contrast to the types of teacher earlier kinds of ITT tried to produce, the missionaries of civil religion, the cultivated teachers sought by liberal educators, and the transformers of society, the Conservative reforms concentrated on providing effective teachers by a greater concentration on subject knowledge and specific teaching competencies rather than theories or disciplines of education, and by transferring control over teaching practice from HEIs to schools. This is not to suggest that others preferred ineffectiveness, or that Conservative governments did not want schools which promoted civic virtue, teachers who were cultivated or schools which encouraged some types of social transformation, even if very different in character from those sought by the New Left, but to note that Conservative priorities became highly pragmatic and instrumental.

New Right critiques

The pace of Conservative reform of teacher education accelerated after the mid-1980s and was more rapid under John Major than Margaret Thatcher. Early caution may be attributed in part to the tendency of Keith Joseph to delay action until every facet of a problem had been fully considered. Margaret Thatcher said in 1987, in reply to a caller on a radio programme

> In many ways, I wish we had begun to tackle education earlier. We had been content to continue with the policies of our predecessors. But now we have much worse left-wing Labour local authorities than we have ever had before - so something simply has to be done.[112]

---

112 Reported in *The Guardian*, 11 June 1987.

The later acceleration of the pace of reform may have owed something to reaction against the negativity and intransigence of the education industry to earlier proposals, a feeling that the Tories might as well be hanged for a sheep as for a lamb. Dissatisfaction with slow progress expressed by intellectuals labelled the 'New Right' also had some effect on ministers. The attacks on this New Right were not very different in kind from those launched earlier against the Black Paper authors, but the New Right caused even more anger on the Left because its ideas seemed to influence governmental policies.

Influential New Right publications included a 1986 pamphlet by the Hillgate Group entitled *Whose Schools? A Radical Manifesto* and a successor in 1987 called *The Reform of British Education: From Principles to Practice*. The Hillgate Group demanded the rapid demolition of the existing structure of teacher education. They rejected the relevance of educational theory to ITT, arguing that 'teaching like business is a form of practical knowledge and may be as much destroyed as enhanced by the attempt to impart it as a theoretical discipline'.[113] They held that the best judges of teaching ability among student teachers or beginning teachers are head teachers and experienced teachers who know intimately the specific conditions in which the teaching takes place. They declared that 'in place of the graduate system we propose a system of working apprenticeship, during which the teacher would receive a salary, and also learn the art of communicating with children in the circumstances most likely to engender it'.

Stuart Sexton favoured 'a shift away from educational theory to the skill of teaching children ... by observing their tutors in a real classroom with real children',[114] although whether he would also maintain that the whole of economics is best learned through shopping, bank transactions, running a business and other practical activities, or surgery by observation and imitation of master surgeons, is unlikely. A 'shift away from educational theory' could easily slip, of course, into a denial that educational theory had any value at all. Anthony O'Hear argued

---

113 Hillgate Group (1986). *Whose Schools? A Radical Manifesto*, p. 15. The co-authors were Caroline Cox, Jessica Douglas-Home, John Marks, Lawrence Norcross and Roger Scruton.
114 Sexton, S. (1987). *Our Schools: A Radical Policy*. London: Institute of Economic Affairs, p. 20.

that successful teaching depends on 'knowledge how rather than knowledge what, and like any other practical knowledge was best acquired in and through experience and doing, rather than through talking and thinking abstractly'.[115] O'Hear, however, differentiated between necessary and sufficient causes, and accepted that it was worthwhile for teachers to study educational ideas and theories 'if only as a prophylactic against the vagaries of educational fashion'. The Hillgate Group seemed not to make that distinction when they argued that 'all key decisions in the scheme [an extension of the Licensed Teacher system] – who is to enrol, how to train, who is to qualify – would be in the hands of experienced teachers whose schools will flourish or decline depending on the quality of the teaching staff they employ'.[116] Of course, teachers on the spot understand much about a school that a visiting lecturer sees only dimly, if at all, yet, in judging student teachers, there may also be much value in seeing regularly a range of their peers in conditions which make very different demands. This is part of the justification for the existence of TTA and OFSTED. Given that the Hillgate Group was profoundly dissatisfied with the professional standards of many teachers as well as those of teacher educators, it seemed strange that they had confidence in teachers' judgements of student teachers.

Sheila Lawlor proved a determined critic of the HEIs. She seemed convinced that the study of education theory, however conceived, was at best useless and more often than not worse than useless. She declared

> Whereas the individual subjects that teachers teach require academic study, the skills of teaching are essentially practical ones. They can only be acquired through experience, trial and error and careful, individual supervision.[117]

She added that 'it is no less foolish to suppose [of a beginning teacher] that the study of educational theory will make him able to teach'. Her view mirrored that developed by some

---

115 O'Hear, A. (1988). *Who Teaches The Teachers?* London: Social Affairs Unit, p. 7.
116 Hillgate Group (1988). *New Teacher in School*, p. 19.
117 Lawlor, S. (1990). *Teachers Mistaught*. London: Centre for Policy Studies, p. 3.

neo-Marxists and radical constructivists about the way children learn: they held that children should be left to make their own discoveries through inquiry and trial and error, unconstrained by teachers' general scientific or analogous theories; and she held that teachers should likewise be left to make their own discoveries unconstrained by general ideas about purposes and methods of education.[118] Lawlor gave its failure to enable student teachers to control disruptive classes as an example of the uselessness of theory, but, although it may have been true that many teacher educators gave advice of very dubious value and that experience is of immense value in promoting orderly and busy classrooms, it is surely false to suppose that the experiences of many others, embedded in general educational ideas, are irrelevant to classroom control.

Lawlor claimed that 'a move to on-the-job training for all graduates would improve the quality of applicant teachers and encourage good qualified graduates to enter the profession ... the colleges and institutes ... should have no more to do with teacher training'.[119] She argued that 'modish educational theory' not only 'deters good graduate specialists from entering the profession', but also that it 'undermines the subject specialism of those who do'. She may be right that many more good graduates would enter teaching if there were no requirement to undertake teacher training first, but she provided no evidence that methods lecturers undermine subject specialism. By and large methods specialists were recruited from able teachers in schools who had further studied the pedagogy of their subjects and/or carried out further substantive study. One of the negative effects of the movement towards school-based ITT is that methods work is now largely in the hands of the teacher of average capacity, rather than those of lecturers, many of whom were initially appointed because they were considered to be particularly able and successful teachers. There is a huge difference between urging that there should be a wider variety of ways of entering teaching and demanding that the main paths used hitherto should be dug up. Critics of the New Right concentrated on denouncing the Lawlor anti-market/anti-choice policy in ITT and implied it was widely held by Conservatives. In practice

---

118 For 'radical constructivism' see Lawlor, 1990, pp. 85–86.
119 Lawlor, 1990, p. 38.

Conservative governments, although opening up new routes of entry, did not abolish, although they certainly changed, the existing routes.

Responses within ITT to Conservative reforms

Teacher education organisations such as UCET opposed every change the Conservatives tried to implement after 1979. A key tactic in opposing changes proposed or effected by Conservative governments was to label them as politically extremist and emanating from a New Right which was pursuing a 'secret agenda', which was not, however, too secret, since its critics were satisfied they had penetrated its lowest depths. Tony Edwards of the University of Newcastle School of Education warned that every Conservative government proposal 'had to be placed in the context of a systematically hostile campaign from the political Right and of a sequence of reforms designed to promote more school-based, school-centred and school-provided training'.[120] He added that 'responding to particular government proposals has been all the more difficult because their relatively moderate form is seen as barely concealing very immoderate intentions'. Stuart Maclure, once editor of the *Times Educational Supplement,* postulated a 'sinister sub-plot' designed to 'take teacher training out of the universities and colleges and ultimately to sever the connection between the study of education in higher education and its practice in schools'.[121] Maclure wrote later that when Kenneth Baker 'gave key jobs on the curriculum and assessment advisory bodies to his friends, there were protests from the world of education echoed by the Opposition in Parliament. It seemed to many obviously unsatisfactory to let party politics loose on the content of school subjects like English and history'.[122]

---

120 Edwards, T. (1994). 'The Universities Council for the Education of Teachers: Defending an Interest or Fighting a Cause' in *Journal of Education for Teaching*, 20 (2), p. 145.
121 *Times Educational Supplement*, 18 June 1993.
122 Maclure, S. (1998). 'Through the Revolution and Out the Other Side' in *Oxford Review of Education,* 24 (1), pp. 15–16. This was a special issue of the *Oxford Review of Education* edited by Maclure. Oxford University had, of course, earlier proved its non-political character by refusing to confer an honorary degree on a woman graduate who had gained some fame in the outside world, one Margaret Thatcher.

Many educationists of the New Left were virulent in their denunciation of those within higher education who criticised their policies. Attacks on the scholarly standing and good faith of their critics were common. Few critics were attacked with more virulence than Brian Cox, Professor of English at the University of Manchester and Joint Editor of *The Black Papers*. For several years Cox gave as good as he got and it was no surprise in 1987, when Kenneth Baker appointed the Kingman Committee of Inquiry into the Teaching of the English Language, that Cox was chosen as chairman of its offshoot, the National Curriculum English Working Group. The Kingman Report and the National Curriculum English Working Group's more detailed recommendations represented a significant movement away from NATE progressive orthodoxy: Sir John Kingman's Committee advocated the teaching of Standard English and was anxious that children should be adequately initiated into rules and conventions of language. However, it did not recommend a return to formal grammar lessons of the pre-1960s type and Brian Cox was accused by former allies, such as John Rae, the recently retired headmaster of Westminster School, of adopting too much of the NATE approach they considered had undermined English teaching in ITT and in the schools.

Margaret Thatcher expressed disappointment that 'the traditional learning of grammar and learning by heart, which I consider vital for memory training, seemed to find no favour' with the Kingman Committee, but she considered its recommendations a step in the right direction, even if an insufficient one. She suggested that 'the fact that many critics considered the direction of these recommendations to be controversial demonstrated just how far things had deteriorated in many classrooms'.[123] Brian Cox may have grown weary of being the object of brutal attacks from within the world of education since the first *Black Papers* years and was seduced by the new pleasurable sensation of receiving some praise from NATE and other circles that had been so hostile in the past may have made him less willing than he might otherwise have been to conciliate old friends who were now his critics. On the other hand he genuinely believed that the Hillgate Group failed to appreciate that there were some constructive features in the approaches

---

123 Thatcher, 1993, p. 595.

advocated by NATE.[124] Yet he must have had mixed feelings when receiving a glowing tribute from Tim Pound of Westminster College, Oxford, who prefaced his praise by labelling the Black Papers 'infamous' and 'generally vilified'.[125]

Despite his pleasure at Brian Cox's change of heart, Dr Pound expressed disgust that an elected government should engage in 'undemocratic manoeuverings' and a 'subversive enterprise' by appointing to committees some members who share some of its views. Pound alleged that Dr John Marenbon was made a member of the School Examinations and Assessment Council and chairman of its English committee 'because of his affiliation to a right-wing think tank, the Centre for Policy Studies'. Had Marenbon been a teacher educator in Westminster College, Oxford, rather than an English don in Trinity College, Cambridge, would his professional knowledge then have been dismissed as irrelevant to consideration of the English curriculum in schools? How much better if the Conservatives had continued to give all these posts to their enemies who, like Maclure and Pound, were clearly above partisanship!

Insight into thinking within UCET is provided by a 1995 article in *Journal of Education for Teaching*, 'The Universities Council for the Education of Teachers: The Facilitator's Tale: A *JET* Colloquy with Mary Russell', jointly devised by Peter Gilroy, Mary Russell and Edgar Stones. Mary Russell was for many years the sole full time member of UCET's staff, while Edgar Stones of the University of Birmingham School of Education and Peter Gilroy of the University of Sheffield School of Education were then editor and deputy editor respectively of *JET*. Sitting in a conclave united by detestation of Conservative policies, the participants are given the names of Froebel, Makarenko, Comenius, Dewey, Montesorri, Erasmus and even Plato. Opposed to these august minds are pitiful ignoramuses. To Gilroy *et al.* the significance of James Callaghan's 1979 Ruskin College speech was that 'our weakness' [that of teacher education organisations] has been to assume 'that rational arguments will win the day … This has not been the way the government has worked in the past and, probably less and less

---

124 See Cox, B. (1992). *The Great Betrayal: Memoirs of a Life in Education*. London: Chapman, ch. 12.
125 Pound, T. (1996). 'Standard English, Standard Culture?' in *Oxford Review of Education*, 22 (2), p. 237.

so now'.¹²⁶ Many politicians and, indeed, other unauthorised intruders into the arcane world of teacher education, are held by politically correct insiders to be incapable of rational argument, so that debate with them is pointless.

'Dewey' remarks in the *JET* Colloquy, 'I remember being at a UCET Conference where UCET discussed whether the viewpoints of 'O'Hare (sic), Cox, Lawlor and others were worth criticising in public and it was agreed that to do so would give them a spurious respectability'.¹²⁷ 'Comenius' added 'I was talking to Eminence Gris the other day and he was convinced that O'Hare had some sort of hold over someone at the very top of the Conservative Party because there cannot be any rational justification for the ideas he was putting about'.¹²⁸ Mary Russell was aghast that CATE's membership included 'people like a journalist from the Financial Times and someone from Kodak'.¹²⁹ UCET may believe in 'power to the people', but not to the wrong sort of people.

The title of an article in *JET* in 1992 by Peter Gilroy is 'The Political Rape of Initial Teacher Education in England and Wales'.¹³⁰ The polemical title was matched by the contents of the article. Dr Gilroy alleged that 'professional educators' had 'recently been faced with a torrent of unjustified abuse' from Conservative Ministers, the press and 'right-wing think-tanks'. This had been a 'grotesquely uninformed attack' by 'Philistines', such as the Centre for Policy Studies, the Hillgate Group and the Social Affairs Unit. These presumptuous bodies 'had begun

---

126 Gilroy, P., Russell, M. and Stones, E. (1995). 'The Universities Council for the Education of Teachers: The Facilitator's Tale: A *JET* Colloquy with Mary Russell' in *Journal of Education for Teaching*, 21 (2), pp. 129–130.
127 Gilroy *et al*. 1995, p. 131.
128 No reference is provided in the notes to this Colloquy for the identity of 'O'Hare' (so spelled throughout the article) who possessed 'some hold' over a leading Conservative, but it may be that Anthony O'Hear was the intended object of attack. O'Hear appears in Reid and Jones, 1997, consistently as 'O'Heare'. The politician over whom 'O'Hare' was thought to have had a hold was perhaps Kenneth Clarke who, according to 'Comenius', made 'an infamous speech to the North of England Education Conference of 1992' or perhaps John Patten, castigated as responsible for the 'farce' of 'Mum's Army'.
129 Gilroy *et al.,* 1995, p. 132.
130 Gilroy, D. P. (1992). 'The Political Rape of Initial Teacher Education in England and Wales' in *Journal of Education for Teaching*, 18 (1), pp. 5–21.

a campaign of ill-informed criticism of teachers and their education, their headline-grabbing assertions finding a ready market in the press'. In Gilroy's view the Philistines operate from 'such an astonishing base of ignorance that publishing a refutation can be seen as dignifying the claims with a spurious respectability'. Some Philistines had somehow infiltrated the sacred groves of academe, such as Anthony O'Hear, but he was dismissed by Gilroy as 'ignorant of the conventions of rational discussion', so there seemed little point dignifying his arguments with the thorough refutation readily available to Gilroy. As part of their account of the introduction of the National Curriculum in Music, John Shepherd and Graham Vulliamy claimed that the parties in dispute 'were made up, not of academics, but of musicians and music educators on the one hand and Conservative politicians and their allies on the other', whose contributions were 'of a highly ideological character'.[131] But few contributors were as ideologically driven as Shepherd and Vulliamy, who knew full well that Anthony O'Hear, Roger Scruton and others among their antagonists were academics, indeed professors, but tried to deny them academic status.[132]

During my visit to Britain in 1997 I had the opportunity to interview David Gilroy, together with Len Barton, at the University of Sheffield. Many of the points they made won my assent. For example they asserted the contestability of education and feared that in some reconstructed initial training courses only methods are open to discussion, not the ends to which they are only the means. They suggested that rapid change and reorganisation can be unsettling and demoralising, deplored excessive central control of education, noting that teacher education is now in a far less autonomous position than other parts of universities, and regretted that some teacher education institutions had weakened their own courses through a system of modules and semesterisation. Len Barton sensibly suggested that a sense of history is needed in teacher education and that

---

131 Shepherd, J. and Vulliamy, G. (1994). 'The Struggle for Culture: a Sociological Case Study of the Development of a National Music Curriculum' in *British Journal of Sociology of Education*, 15 (1), p. 34.
132 See Tooley J. and Darby D. (1998). *Educational Research: A Critique – A Survey of Published Educational Research*. London: Office for Standards in Education, p. 30.

there is little of it in most ITT courses in Britain at present. His own suggestion that Raymond Williams' *The Long Revolution* would help to provide a broader perspective is entirely sensible, but one would hope that Williams on the Left might be supplemented by other points of view.[133] It was partly because alternative perspectives were so rarely presented in teacher education in the past, when more time was devoted to 'disciplines of education', that educational theory fell into discredit.

Another educationist who seemed to regard contrary thought as outside the realms of debate was Eric Bolton. Soon after he had ceased to be the senior Chief Inspector of Schools in the ranks of HMI to become a luminary of teacher education, Professor Bolton told the Council of LEAs in Liverpool in July 1992:

> Particularly saddening is the re-emergence of the search for a workable form of selection and segregation. There is no evidence that bears scrutiny that shows that standards of achievement at the end of secondary schooling have generally fallen ... Questions and debates about how to segregate pupils into academic and non-academic, vocational and non-vocational, practical and theoretical sheep and goats, at as early an age as 14, are not only irrelevant but downright counterproductive. Even worse is the call by the Prime Minister that we should return to a system of examining at the end of compulsory schooling that by design sets out to qualify only 25 per cent of pupils.[134]

Quite apart from the crude misrepresentation of John Major's argument, it was most arrogant to seek to exclude even the Prime Minister of the day from public discussion about some key educational issues.

The strong dislike of teacher education organisations for OFSTED and the TTA was sometimes expressed as though it were part of a consistent and principled opposition to greater concentration of educational power and authority. Tony Edwards,

---

133 Raymond Williams' biographer, Fred Inglis, who has held two chairs in teacher education, applauded him for denouncing '... Them, the thing, the bosses, capitalism, weaponry, human indifference, vulgar self-indulgence, global poisoning, family betrayal, class disloyalty'. Yet, despite his advocacy of equality and denunciations of cultural elitism, Williams sent his own children to independent schools.
134 *Times Educational Supplement*, 31 July 1992.

for example, argued that since 1984 'teacher education has been a conspicuous example of increasing state centralism in education'. Yet several Conservative changes which gave greater power to schools and their own heads and governors received no praise from UCET, whereas the massive educational changes imposed by the Wilson Labour governments from 1964 to 1979, had been acclaimed by the most influential educational organisations. There were no complaints when the Schools Council was packed with leading lights of the educational Left, but Professor Edwards was apparently shocked when CATE was established, because it was 'given a membership progressively reformed to secure a strong voice for overt opponents of the "educational establishment" i.e. education departments, only to be replaced ... by a Training Agency even more closely tied to the Secretary of State's wishes and agenda'. UCET was not opposed to central control as such, but wanted it to be exercised by educational professionals, with a General Teaching Council a favourite proposal. It frequently referred to teachers as a collectivity capable of establishing standards of professional competence, although many teachers join a professional organisation mainly for protection if they are accused of unprofessional practices or sub-professional standards.

UCET greeted suggestions that success as a teacher must be judged in part at least in terms of pupils' learning by shocked references to Robert Lowe's 1862 Revised Code and 'payment by results', and claims that adequate allowance can never be made for huge differences in contexts of teaching. If this were so it would disqualify almost all talk about excellence in teaching or success in ITT. 'Value-added' modes of assessment enable reliable estimates to be made of teachers' contributions to students' learning, conduct and overall progress, taking into account their starting points and influences external to schools. This approach is to be sure difficult to apply to ITT, since student teachers do not 'own' a classroom as do regular teachers, but appropriate techniques can be applied informally as the basis for part of their assessment of the evaluation of their practical teaching.

Most educational follies are based on half-truths or elevation of a single truth to the status of the only relevant truth. This has happened in assessment and evaluation. It is true that some important sorts of understanding are not easily quantified or measured, and that refined judgements of quality can be made only by people with a depth of relevant knowledge. For example, it is easy to provide rules for writing a sonnet and to reject verse forms that do not meet the clear criteria for their production, but there is no mechanical or quantitative method whereby one can distinguish between Shakespeare's 'Shall I compare thee to a summer's day?' and sheer banality. Yet this truth does not make literary criticism impossible. When education, like literature or the theatre in this respect, is in a healthy condition, interested outsiders are generally willing to accept criteria of merit employed by apparently expert insiders, although they naturally want such criteria to be made as clear as possible. At times, however, a field is taken over by groups whose criteria and/or methods of application seem bizarre and unconvincing to concerned outsiders. Sometimes it seems that no coherent criteria are being applied. This situation was created in education by the New Left and the only short-term solution Conservative governments thought they had at their disposal was to split teaching into a large number of specific activities which seemed readily amenable to objective appraisal. That mechanical checklist systems cannot adequately evaluate higher levels of quality has been used by root-and-branch opponents of educational assessment as grounds for not employing them at all. However, the defect of such systems is not that they are of no use whatsoever, but that they cannot do what is most required in judgements of educational achievement. Simple competency checks can be a valuable feature of quality control in education, but they are not sufficient in themselves to evaluate the extent to which many higher important educational objectives are being attained.

UCET received wide support for its opposition to Conservative reforms to ITT from the education industry as a whole, including not only the more militant unions but also the traditionally more moderate Association of Teachers and Lecturers (ATL).[135] In 1997 ATL published *A Critique of the National Curriculum for Initial Teacher Training*, commissioned from Professor Colin Richards, formerly a senior HMI, and Paul Harling and David Webb of the University College of St Martin,

---

135 The ATL was formerly the AMMA (Assistant Masters and Mistresses Association), itself a merger between the Assistant Masters Association and the Assistant Mistresses Association.

Lancaster. Richards *et al.* condemned the National Curriculum for ITT on the grounds that 'little or no recognition is given in the circulars to the importance of critically examining the meaning and purpose of education, understanding child development, holding up the school National Curriculum to critical scrutiny or to studying the social, cultural and ethical dimensions of teaching and learning in primary schools'.[136] However, if the ITT documents had extended the 'standards' to include critical understanding of the meaning and purpose of education, the social, cultural and ethical dimensions of education, and the nature of professional judgement, what an uproar there would then have been against Tory intrusion in even wider areas of educational activity!

Richards *et al.* asserted that the relevant circulars 'fail to recognise the crucial importance of professional understanding and judgement' and contain 'only one element: a detailed specification of the content to be taught', although they conceded that this specification was 'provided in a valuably detailed and direct form'. They condemned the specifications of content for allowing 'scope for a degree of diverse interpretation' and for offering 'no attainment targets, no reference to programmes of study, and no assessment arrangements or specification of levels of achievement. They questioned the wisdom of confining the National Curricula requirements for teacher education to 'the "core" subjects of English, mathematics and (next year) science'. They also asked 'why there is no intention to spell out the training requirements of the remaining seven subjects of the school National Curriculum and of religious education?' and demanded to know, 'are there no essential elements in these subjects which all teacher trainees ought to be taught'.[137] Yet the National Curriculum for schools was also savagely criticised by professional educators for over-burdening teachers and as excessively intrusive because it did provide attainment targets, references to programmes of study, and assessment arrangements and specifications of levels of achievement.

Richards *et al.* implied that if teachers are prepared to become 'skilled technicians' who can provide 'basic instruction',

---

136 Richards, C., Harling, P. and Webb, D. (1997). *A Key Stage 6 Core Curriculum?: A Critique of the National Curriculum for Initial Teacher Training* (London, Association of Teachers and Lecturers), p. 2.
137 Richards *et al.*, 1997, p. 5.

this somehow inhibits them from becoming 'imaginative, creative teachers whose informed professional judgement leads to intelligent action'[138] but this implication showed a failure to distinguish between necessary and sufficient conditions. In any case, the TTA's own QTS document stated clearly that the professional standard it seeks to promote 'implies more than meeting a series of discrete standards. It is necessary to consider standards as a whole to appreciate the creativity, commitment, energy and enthusiasm which teaching demands, and the intellectual and managerial skills required of the effective professional'.

Morton's Fork was applied ferociously in attacks on Conservative reforms. On the one hand the National Curriculum was attacked as draconian and highly intrusive, but on the other hand condemned as superfluous, since its requirements were already carried out almost universally. Richards *et al.* argued that in respect of primary education, 'in relation to English and mathematics specifically, few institutions will need to radically redesign courses, because there is remarkably little in the proposed ITT curriculum which is not implied by the documents which already govern the preparation of primary teachers'.[139]

Frequently during the Conservative years after 1979, the organisations representing teacher educators first denounced governmental changes, subsequently accepted them through rank-and-file pressure, but continued to oppose new proposals for change as stridently as before. Richards *et al.* made several key admissions about the defensibility and success of Conservative reforms which had earlier been denounced within the education industry. For example, Richards *et al.* accepted that the 1982 Report by HMI which revealed that about a quarter of newly-qualified primary teachers were insecure in subjects they were teaching was at least 'partly justified',[140] although both the 1982 Report and DES Circular 3/84 to which it gave rise were denounced at the time as teacher bashing. A 1996 article jointly authored by six leading teacher educators, including some fierce critics of Conservative policies, conceded that

---

138 Richards *et al.*, 1997, p. 26.
139 Richards *et al.*, 1997, p. 24.
140 Richards *et al.*, 1997, p. 3.

their 'fieldwork revealed that virtually all secondary courses and the vast majority of primary courses in the Spring of 1995 claimed either to be working in partnership with schools or in the final stages of transition'.[141]

Regrettably, even when teacher or teacher education organisations changed their own ground, they rarely admitted to any significant defects in the 1979 structure of ITT, nor retracted earlier accusations of bad faith against Conservative governments and their supposed advisers. Labour politicians were more likely than teacher education organisations to concede publicly that past policies favoured by the Left were seriously flawed. Neil Fletcher, for example, Labour Leader of the ILEA, expressed in 1987 his fears that 'mixed ability and progressive teaching methods have failed to equip children with basic skills of literacy and numeracy' and claimed that many parents were full of 'concern about spelling, concern about handwriting, concern about homework, even just simple things like learning poetry, the old ways of absorbing culture, hymn singing, all the things that used to happen'.[142] Such sentiments would have virtually precluded appointment in many schools and departments of Education.

---

141 Furlong, J., Whitty, G., Whiting, W., Miles, S., Barton, L. and Barrett, E. (1996). Redefining Partnership: Revolution or Reform in Initial Teacher Education? in *Journal of Education for Teaching,* 22 (1), p. 41.
142 *Sunday Times*, 1 November 1987.

4 | My 1997 Interviews

My initial limited intention in my 1997 interviews was to find out whether the almost uniform hostility shown to the Conservative reform programme in ITT by official organisations reflected genuine sentiments among teacher educators who had recently written about changes involving their own institutions. I did not need to come to England to learn that there had been massive changes in teacher education since 1979 when Margaret Thatcher became Prime Minister, the most important being that ITT as a whole was controlled nationally by OFSTED and the TTA, the balance of power over teaching practice had moved from HEIs to schools, more time was spent within ITT on teaching practice at the expense of HEI-based courses, time spent in theoretical studies within ITT, the establishment of a National Curriculum for ITT supervised by the TTA, and that within the HEI courses time devoted to the disciplines of education or generic educational ideas had been transferred to subject-based curricular and pedagogic studies. However, extended discussions with practitioners seemed the best way to judge how successful and effective, if at all, any of these changes had been in their own eyes.

Attitudes towards OFSTED and the TTA

Zealous minorities are usually highly over-represented in conferences and committees of professional organisations, but my interviews suggested that many teacher educators in 1997 shared the dislike of OFSTED and the TTA expressed by UCET. OFSTED and TTA were described as unfairly searching out weaknesses, nominally 'in the name of improvement', but really 'to make sure fault is found'. Jim Campbell of Warwick University considered OFSTED too fault-finding and insufficiently constructive. The consequence of excessive harshness and negativity, it was often claimed, was that anxieties are unnecessarily increased, with many early retirements and much mental illness. Some teacher educators felt they were scapegoats and whipping-boys. At Bristol University Malcolm Lewis complained of high opportunity costs of the new system: as PGCE co-ordinator, he himself had to spend most of his time in administrative duties relating to partnerships with schools, with heads, mentors, even school governors. Yet Dr Lewis, like Frank Hardman of Newcastle University, also felt that HEIs receive insufficient feedback from OFSTED. Dr Lewis also complained that TTA often made late changes to its requirements and then demanded almost immediate compliance, resulting in frustration and anger at having constantly to be reactive. He considered it would be better if inspection came in one spell across all subjects, like the old general inspection by HMI, rather than as 'drip-feed' throughout the year: Bristol University School of Education had three OFSTED subject inspections in 1996 and five in 1997, with the remaining subject to be inspected in 1998. However, other informants preferred to have inspection in separate phases, since one group of subject lecturers often learned how best to cope with inspection from colleagues who had already gone through the process.

Even though their ranks include several teacher educators on part-time duty, as well as head teachers and other senior school staff, OFSTED inspectors were described by one lecturer as 'all suits' who possess a 'mechanistic version of modernity' and apply 'simple mechanistic measures'. Terry Martin of Southampton University was critical of the aspirations of some OFSTED inspectors, whom he accused of engaging in an unrealistic search for perfection, in which the best soon became the enemy of the good, since the stress and strain created actually reduced the efficiency of teacher educators and their students. Some staff at Manchester Metropolitan University (MMU) held that OFSTED inspectors are often chosen because of their history of hostility to teacher education. Several teacher educators believed that SCITT schools were excused the worst of inspection and that this is very unfair. David Reid of Manchester University considered that the scaling system used by TTA was unfair, being much harsher on teacher educators than on schools. He argued that, although TTA's emphasis on professional qualifications seems laudable on the surface, there was an insidious hidden agenda. He suggested that the Conservatives had deliberately dumbed down teacher education, so that future teachers would be unable to mount an adequate theoretical challenge to governments. He claimed that many teacher educators felt they had to tell students the National Curriculum is fine, even though they considered it basically misconceived, as he did himself, since doubts in students' minds might undermine their ability to teach the curriculum well.

Jack Hogbin, Quality Manager at the Didsbury School of Education of MMU, considered there were fundamental disagreements between many teacher educators and the TTA, founded on different philosophies of teaching held by each party and dispute about the ways in which key principles (often shared) have been put into practice. Behind these disagreements, he held, lay a 'political' judgement by the TTA that teacher educators have been responsible for letting standards drift. Jack Hogbin claimed that the accusation of low standards was not justified and that the need to raise standards was exaggerated for political reasons. A frequently expressed fear was that OFSTED inspection was of so intrusive a character as to undermine the autonomy of teacher education and thus to lead other faculties to wish to remove ITT completely from universities, since the trend to greater external control might spread into other areas.

Several teacher educators disliked the TTA's practice of classifying an entire HEI as non-compliant if one of its students recommended for a pass on teaching subsequently failed inspection. Lecturers in MMU Didsbury College were aggrieved that TTA had insisted in 1996 on inspecting the two separate schools of education in MMU, Didsbury and Crewe, as a single unit with a combined grade for subjects taught in both campuses. They claimed that weaknesses at Crewe led to an unfair downgrading of their courses as well. On the other hand it could be argued that harsh medicine of this sort was needed to remedy weaknesses, if such there really were in the Crewe campus, as they implied. That four out of eighteen institutions first inspected by TTA were found lacking and severely penalised was adduced as evidence of the unfairness of the inspection procedures, although the generally low level of failure was also seen as an endorsement of the quality achieved by teacher educators. Frank Hardman feared that the new system forces teacher education institutions into destructive competition, with the result that there is little sharing of experiences between them as there had been in the past, although my own recollections of working in teacher education in the 1960s and 1970s do not include much in the way of such sharing of experiences.

Chris Woodhead was often a special target of criticism. Some lecturers I interviewed accused him of manipulating statistics, including SATs, twisting Circular 14/93, and trying to entrap teacher educators by encouraging the asking of loaded questions to young teachers about their competency training during ITT. Some lecturers believed that Woodhead had been displeased when most primary courses inspected in 1994 received favourable assessment and had responded by increasing demands, particularly in literacy, to ensure that more courses would fail to meet the standards. David Reid believed that the Tories deliberately excluded teacher educators from quangos on teacher education.

Yet, despite these severe attacks on Conservative policies and the way in which OFSTED and the TTA carried them out, almost all the teacher educators I met were insistent that their own institutions were in good shape. Although several claimed that many teacher educators were looking for other jobs, in schools, academic writing or PhD study, none suggested that the quality of teacher education staff had suffered any decline. Many in fact claimed there had been big improvements since the pre-1979 era. Terry Martin held that the TTA total package was good in concept, although applied too harshly. John Furlong suggested that the problem with TTA was not that any specific demand it made was unreasonable in itself, but that the mode of inspection had been too draconian, whereas milder forms of government intervention had been applied in Wales, Scotland and Northern Ireland. Furlong considered that the pattern in the United States of numerous private universities and great variation even within the state universities and colleges might have been a better model for British Conservatives to try to emulate, rather than uniformity controlled by central government.

David Reid held that vice-chancellors were often 'less than impressed' by the high costs to teacher education of the new partnership arrangements, but he added 'to be honest we are better off now' than in the past, in the sense that the schools have given more professional commitment since they were acknowledged to be and paid as genuine partners in teacher education. He thought that schools of Education were also better off because the TTA had 'ring fenced' much of their income which in the past vice-chancellors could cream off. David Reid's own department used its School Support Tutors as a 'mini-OFSTED' and devised questionnaires based on TTA circulars to check on compliance, because they provided a helpful check-list of desirable attributes.

David Lambert, Secondary Co-ordinator in London University Institute of Education, credited OFSTED and TTA with forcing attention to black spots which were often insufficiently dealt with in the past and with emphasising the need for adequate subject knowledge, improved assessment techniques, and school-based research, although he considered their mode of operation as punitive and based on a deficit model, with excessive penalties for minimal non-compliance and too much emphasis on negatives in press releases. Richard Beare of the University of Warwick believed the powers of TTA to be too draconian, but conceded that until its inception there had been too much *laissez-faire* and a lot of sloppy work in ITT. Other lecturers made the point that the National Curriculum for ITT had changed attitudes to slack colleagues very considerably. Whereas, even in the recent past, HEIs simply waited for the idle to retire, perhaps encouraging that step by a financial inducement, the policy of TTA of downgrading all courses if there is total failure in just one key requirement in the new ITT curriculum had greatly increased pressures on slack or incompetent staff. Increased pressures may sometimes have overtaxed conscientious lecturers, but in the past teacher educators strenuously maintained they already worked under severe pressures. My overall impression was that many teacher educators considered that the TTA had succeeded in raising levels of efficiency in their own and other HEIs, but that the benefits achieved could have been gained by gentler methods.

The new system was condemned by some teacher educators I interviewed, such as Mike Harrison at Manchester University who suggested to me that standards for the National Curriculum for schools had been set on the basis of what might be achieved by a small minority in favourable educational conditions. Harrison compared OFSTED's demands with expecting all children to compose like Beethoven and paint like Picasso, and rejected any universalistic requirements as unrealistic. He considered the demands made on teachers were also unreasonable and wondered why a primary teacher who can, say, show children the meaning of the paintings of Lowry, should be expected to be able to teach geography as well? On the other hand he held that primary age children need to have a single class teacher in order to feel secure.

John Furlong was very critical of the listing of numerous specific competences, each of which has to be certified by TTA inspectors by a tick in the appropriate box as having been achieved. David Lambert welcomed the movement away from competences to standards in the approach of TTA, but feared it may be only a cosmetic change. However, when used intelligently and providing it is understood that they do not express in entirety what it means to become a good teacher, he believed that the standards help beginning teachers and co-tutors analyse teaching and learning, and enable them to set specific targets for improvement.

Several teacher educators I interviewed strongly supported the TTA's approach to competency and standards. Jerry Norton of Sunderland University School of Education considered that the introduction of the National Curriculum for ITT had led to greater emphasis on expertise in particular subjects or skills, such as reading or mathematics, and reduced concern in primary ITT with integration by topic and centre of interest and inter-disciplinary approaches, and that in general both primary and secondary students are better prepared than in the past for the demands of classrooms. Lecturers in Plymouth University School of Education maintained that at the end of their courses beginning teachers were more articulate and sophisticated than a decade ago, more aware of formal demands of teaching, and more keen and committed than a decade ago, although they have higher anxiety levels. Some staff in MMU held that beginning teachers had a significantly higher skill level than their predecessors a generation ago and consider current courses to be much more structured and better able to meet the new Key Skills 2 requirements. By 1998 some formerly fierce critics of Conservative policies had tacked in the face of changed opinions among many of their colleagues. David Hartley, a New Left educator, was willing to concede in 1998 that 'the initial move towards competence-based and school-based training – such as that pioneered at the University of Oxford – was made for sound *pedagogic* reasons', although he went on to suggest that 'it appears to have been co-opted by the former Conservative government for *political* reasons (emphasis as in original).[143] The poor old Tories could not win a trick. Even if there were sound pedagogic reasons for anything they did, their motives were necessarily dishonest, so they deserve no credit. Of course, failures on their part to introduce whatever a David Hartley might advocate were even more reprehensible.

Roger Trend of Exeter University has argued that there are 'some clear benefits of the standards to formal teacher training' introduced by the TTA, such as:

- It permits focused and structured (i.e. deliberate) attention to a wide range of issues.

- It reduces the risk of important but less visible items skipping through the training curriculum net.

- It allows national standards to be established and monitored by external agencies.

- It provides a framework for reporting progress and attainment of QTS to the profession.

- It goes some way to ensuring consistency and reliability of assessment whatever the route to QTS.[144]

Trend claimed that the standards approach does not necessarily preclude 'a host of other things happening' which teacher educators or mentor teachers in schools might wish to further. There is, of course, a danger that achievement of a particular cut-off standard may lead young teachers to consider they have no further progress to make in that dimension of teaching, and many teacher educators are rightly worried about a tendency for 'plateauing' to take place. Yet, once those dangers are understood, steps can be taken to guard against them.

Trend's most incisive criticism of the QTS statements was that 'as they stand they give very little indication of performance level'. He provided as an example the requirement to be able to 'monitor and intervene when teaching to ensure sound learning and discipline'. He noted that 'this standard raises a number of questions, such as "how sound?", "how often?", "with

---

143 Hartley, D. (1998). 'Repeat Prescription: the National Curriculum for Initial Teacher Training' in *British Journal of Educational Studies*, 46 (1), pp. 73–4.
144 Trend, R. (1997). *Qualified Teacher Status: A Practical Introduction*. London: Letts Educational, p. 10.

which pupils?", "with what class sizes?"'. Malcolm Lewis at Bristol University, too, had no opposition to standards in principle, but he observed there was still a lack of effective benchmarks despite a plethora of descriptions of teaching activities. Michael Scriven drew a similar conclusion from a comparable set of standards issued in the United States by the Interstate New Teacher Assessment and Support Consortium. One item was: 'The teacher plans instruction based on knowledge of subject matter, students, the community, and curriculum goals'. Scriven argued that all teachers are almost bound to meet this standard as stated at least minimally, since all know something of the subject matter, the students, the community, and, given an hour in the staffroom library, the curriculum goals.[145] It is hard to see how a general description of an activity in which every teacher is bound to engage, whether well or badly, can act as any guarantee of educational standards. The proper use of the standards is to provide a framework or matrix within which are identified dimensions of a subject which require distinctive attention. Their misuse is to suggest that standards themselves are capable of evaluating quality of thought or performance. Unfortunately, opposition to the standards system from teacher education organisations has generally been based on the claim that standards are not needed at all, not that they are insufficient for qualitative judgement of excellence in teaching.

It is important to ensure that teachers have adequate theoretical understanding of methodology and that they possess, and/or are encouraged to develop, personal qualities which generally foster effective teaching. Yet in both cases correlations are very imperfect. We should ensure that teachers understand which methods generally work well and try to encourage, say, diligence and punctuality. Yet some teachers use the methods which usually work well but get nowhere with their pupils, whereas others who have not compared and contrasted alternative approaches somehow hit on a very good one. Massive research projects have sought to establish relationships between teaching styles or methods on the one hand and pupils' achievements on the other, but with limited success.[146] Overall, the

---

[145] Scriven, M. (1996). 'Assessment in Teacher Education: Getting Clear on the Concept' in *Teaching and Teacher Education,* 12 (4), p 446.
[146] A British 'classic' study is Bennett, N. (1976). *Teaching Styles and Pupil Progress.* London: Open Books.

research literature suggests that highly structured teacher-centred classrooms are more effective than open-ended student-centred ones, but many 'formal' teachers are not very effective, whereas some highly informal ones are highly effective. And some diligent and punctual people prove poor as teachers, whereas some lazy and unpunctual people are very effective once they are in the classroom and put their minds to the job.

Partnerships between HEIs and schools

The gap between UCET and rank-and-file teacher educators proved to be much greater in respect of the new type of partnership between schools and HEIs than of attitudes towards OFSTED and the TTA. The new partnerships, once established, have proved very popular with many teacher educators. University of Newcastle lecturers told me that schools' expectations of student teachers had become much more explicit, especially in regard to conceptions of 'entitlement', than in the past and that there were far closer relationships between mentors and teacher educators, which often leads as well to closer in-service co-operation and facilitates school-based research. They displayed little nostalgia for the pre-1991 situation and considered there had been definite gains in subsequent changes. They consider there is now closer contact between schools and teacher educators, clearer information about duties and roles, and more consistent and thoughtful evaluation of student teachers, whom they consider more conscientious than in the past, with far fewer 'drifters'. They agreed with David Hargreaves that the need for school staffs to co-operate to meet the demands of the National Curriculum has led to greater collegiality than in the 'laissez-faire' past.

Hargreaves examined fears that school-based teacher education was a reversion to the 'pre-technocratic' system' of 'sitting next to Nellie'. He concluded instead that these schemes may constitute a 'post-technocratic model', in which a better balance of theory and practice is generally gained than hitherto. Hargreaves went further and claimed that in the past the typical teacher in Britain could be almost completely an individualist, especially primary teachers who had almost complete control of their 'own' classes, with little or no check on their knowledge of what they taught or failed to teach. He identified a 'new professionalism' which is 'associated with greater professional pride and self-confidence' and claimed there is also much more emphasis now on curriculum continuity and development. This has led schools to engage institutionally in curriculum study and development much more than in the past and has reduced the school–tertiary gap.

Hargreaves considered that the new arrangements on the whole provided 'a much higher quality of support and guidance for the trainee on teaching practice' and 'far better support to new teachers during their first few years in the profession'. He summarised the post-1984 changes as 'a growing synthesis between a more sophisticated conception of professional development and a strong commitment to institutional development'.[147] Hargreaves was confident that 'the trend is clearly for practising teachers to:

- contribute more to the design and planning of course

- be trained for their role, which requires the trainers to share their skills with the mentors

- share in, or even take primary responsibility for, the formal assessment of trainees during the practicum

- in some cases take the primary or even total responsibility for the initial training of teachers'.[148]

In 1992 Kenneth Clarke expressed the case for a shift from HEI to schools in the balance of ITT in forthright terms:

> Theory can be no substitute for this practical training in professions that give person to person service. Student teachers need more time in classrooms guided by serving teachers and less time in the teacher training college.

Yet, as Dennis O'Keeffe has argued, 'if there is intellectually wrong material being transmitted, more practice is actually likely to make matters worse', the result being 'at best effort refined and honed'.[149] It is very true that theory can be no substitute for practical training, but it is equally true that practical training in itself is no substitute for appropriate

---

147 Hargreaves, 1994, p. 424.
148 ibid. p. 432.
149 O'Keeffe, D. (1990). *The Wayward Elite: A Critique of British Teacher Education*. London: The Adam Smith Institute, p. 27.

theory, even in 'person to person' professions such as medicine and education. The key problem about the balance of time in teacher education is assessing what can best be done by observation and practice in classrooms and what by more detached study outside classrooms. Kenneth Clarke's analysis was not notably helpful in getting the balance right, especially since the one thing teachers will get in abundance in their careers is time in classrooms. The real value in Clarke's policies and those of his Conservative colleagues was in providing new modes of ITT which enabled both insiders and outsiders to make informed comparisons between the old and the new, and indeed between different forms of the new.

Lecturers in Sunderland University School of Education gave no credit to the Conservatives for any improvements, any more than wartime Londoners would have given the Luftwaffe credit for increasing social solidarity by launching the blitz, but they held that practicums are now 'enormously more effective' than a few years ago, although further significant improvement is possible. University of Plymouth lecturers claimed that there are now closer links between schools and teacher education than in the past, to the benefit of student teachers and education as a whole. They hold that the new system of 'partnership' is generally effective, and not merely a rhetorical pretence. David Lambert considered that between 1990 and 1997 there had been a big improvement in its partnership with schools. Under their 1997 system a practising teacher is now one of the two interviewers for applicants to the Institute's ITT courses. Like other co-ordinators, Dr Lambert found there is a huge variation in the standard of co-tutors (subject teachers), and to some extent of professional tutor in school (deputy head or another senior figure), but that had always been the case. He believed that the Institute's school tutors generally managed under the current arrangements to maintain a more acceptable level of consistency of experience for the student teachers than in the past. Roger Trend claimed that at Exeter University achievement of greater consistency in assessment of student performance in schools is given high priority in consultations between the university and its over 300 partner schools. Jim Campbell made the point that staff development in large secondary schools is now generally good and that this improvement may be partly the result of schools having a more structured role in ITT and the dominant role in the assessment of practicums.

London University Institute of Education's 1996 *Partnership in Initial Teacher Education: a Topography* asserted that in the new type of partnership there were benefits 'in terms of the increased professionalism of students' training' and 'establishing closer working relationships with schools'. It argued that school teachers' own increased role in ITT was proving a major force for professional development in the schools.[150] David Reid maintained that the 'The Empowerment Model' developed recently by Manchester University as their partnership model with schools was much superior to anything available in the past. John Savin of MMU Didsbury College argued that its new system for co-operation between school mentors and teacher educators was far better than anything available a few years ago. Under this system Tuesdays are always left free by both school and university for mentor–tutor activities with student teachers, with subject issues being dealt with in morning sessions and wider topics in the afternoons. He claimed that the clusters of schools set up by MMU are already beginning to form the basis for significant educational research. John Trafford of Sheffield University considered that the 'awareness and commitment of schools has been raised' in recent years and that personal relationships between school mentors and university staff are better than in the past. The view was frequently expressed that extended responsibility for student teachers and the new partnership arrangements have been powerful forces in stimulating inservice education and extending the theoretical interests of many teachers. Roger Trend emphasised that at Exeter achievement of greater consistency in assessment of student performance in schools was given high priority in consultations between the university and its over 300 partner schools. The University of Plymouth claimed that there were closer links than in the past between schools and teacher education, to the benefit of student teachers and education as a whole.

Most teacher training institutions have partnerships with independent as well as government schools. David Reid is proud of the wide range of schools with which Manchester University has long-term partnerships, stretching from Manchester Grammar School to Duthy Street Secondary School, which

---

150 London University Institute of Education (1996). *Partnership in Initial Teacher Education: a Topography*, p. 69.

offers a large amount of special education. One of the few exceptions has been Oxford University Department of Education, where Professor Richard Pring rejected proffered places for student teachers in Abingdon School, a generally well-regarded independent school, on the grounds that his department wanted to liaise exclusively with local authority comprehensive schools.[151]

Far from denouncing the new partnership system, teacher educators in 1997, such as Malcolm Lewis at Bristol University, were more likely to claim to have advocated such partnerships, even before the Conservatives thought of them! John Furlong took pride in claiming that both Bristol University and Swansea University, where he held his previous appointment, had taken independent steps to establish partnerships before any pressure was applied from above. The strongest claims to be pioneers in partnerships seem, however, to be those of Oxford, Exeter and Sussex Universities.

Not all effects of new partnership arrangements were regarded as beneficial, of course. Now that teachers have officially the leading influence on teaching practice, and there is great pressure on them to fit in with a whole-school response to the National Curriculum, teacher educators have less opportunity to persuade student teachers to adopt any practices that differ significantly from those in the practice school. Under the new partnership arrangement several teacher educators told me that they feel very unsure as to whether they ought to try to exert such an influence, even if time and opportunity were greater.

Dave Heywood of MMU argued that it was difficult to moderate teaching practice honestly and objectively, since there are now fears of adverse consequences if judgements are made different from those of OFSTED inspectors, or of the schools, especially given the difficulties of finding sufficient teaching practice places. David Reid maintained that it is often hard to achieve quality control, but that TTA blames teacher educators if things go wrong. Schools can manage without teacher education providers, but not so the reverse. There are no sanctions university can employ against school, other than to drop it next year, which is itself difficult when school practice places are in

---

151 Letter from the Headmaster of Abingdon School in *The Times*, 27 September 1993.

short supply. Malcolm Lewis noted that teacher educators now find it vital to tread gently with mentors and subject teachers in schools in order to maintain good relationships. He also observed that the universities cannot control the impressions their partner schools give OFSTED of their contribution to the partnerships and that there is often anxiety as to whether the same story is told to all listeners. Bristol University had in 1997 over fifty secondary schools in partnership, with a wide variety of age ranges (11–16, 11–18, 16–18, etc), so that it was very difficult to ensure coherence and consistency, although TTA demands it. TTA regulations demanded that students be allocated only to satisfactory subject departments, but there were many changes in staffing and internal organisation in many schools, taken naturally enough without consulting distant teacher educators. The latter, however, were expected by TTA to exert a form of quality control it is not within their power to achieve, however hard they tried – and if they tried too hard they were accused by many in the schools of arrogant and undue interference.

John Trafford noted that in Sheffield University tutors see students teach only about half as much as they did in the past. Terry Martin expressed regret that teacher educators were now marginalised and in a weak position in attempts to ensure a high quality in school mentors. David Reid claimed that OFSTED was more interested in mentors' debriefing of student teachers than with direct observation in classrooms, so it was hardly surprising that university lecturers have moved in the same direction. Professor Reid added that it is difficult now for teacher educators to help students to prepare lesson plans for school practice and that, indeed, this formerly key responsibility of subject tutors has been formally transferred to the schools under the new partnership system. Malcolm Lewis also regretted the significant reduction in teacher educators' visits to schools in recent years, from typically four or five to now one or two. And whereas in the past visits had normally included direct observation of students' lessons, now this was somewhat rare and concentration was on attending the debriefing of student teachers by mentors. Dave Heywood noted that schools were not obliged to offer teaching practice places, but teacher training institutions were forced to find them. He noted, too the high opportunity costs of OFSTED, which he estimated to be about 6 per cent of total staff time (about £120,000 for MMU) in order to prepare for OFSTED inspection, which thus became an obstacle to improving their performance, not a spur to improvement. In addition the payment of £1,200 a year to schools for each student teacher on practice amounted to £750,000 for MMU.

Many teacher educators were ambivalent in their attitude to the average teacher in the schools. On the one hand they deplore what they claim to be a lack of reflectiveness in many classrooms and staff rooms, yet they are quick with accusations of 'teacher bashing' whenever a politician or any person outside the education industry expresses similar doubts and reservations about teacher quality. David Reid argued that the Conservative emphasis on school-based ITT was irrational because Conservative ministers so frequently attacked teachers in the schools for poor professional standards, but, since those same ministers distrusted the average teacher educator even more, there was some logic to their position.

Overall, however, my informants held that relationships between schools and teacher education has improved as a result of the Conservative reforms and that greater involvement in ITT by teachers had been a big stimulus to professional development. Most of them endorsed the view of William Taylor that the development of school-based teacher education has been 'valid and sensible'.[152] Student teachers' perceptions of the relative importance of schools and universities in ITT have been similar to those of Conservative governments. Cameron-Jones and O'Hara investigated whether students beginning secondary teacher training in Edinburgh considered that school or tertiary education staff would have the greater influence on them during teacher education, schools proved to be preponderant.[153] On six out of ten types of 'professional skill', most students considered that they would be influenced more or less equally by the two; in respect of one item only, 'the way the Scottish education system works', most thought they would learn more from the teacher educators; in respect of three key competences they expected to be the most difficult to achieve they thought schools would be much more significant. These three competencies

---

152 Reported in Gilroy, 1992, p. 13.
153 Cameron-Jones, M. and O'Hara, P. (1995). 'Students' Expectations of Influence on their Competence in Initial Teacher Education' in *Studies in Higher Education*, 20 (3), pp. 329–39.

were classroom communication, classroom management and the way schools work. The attitudes most students in this research expressed deeply depress some educationists, such as F. Feiman-Nemser *et al.*, who seem to consider them to indicate a lack of critical acumen or reflectiveness, but Cameron-Jones and O'Hara were convinced that a new and valuable complementarity between schools and teacher educators was developing.[154]

Educational theory

There has been a significant reduction in the amount of time devoted to educational theory or educational studies in general in ITT over the last 15 years. John Trafford of Sheffield University estimated in our discussions that over 90 per cent of the 12 weeks PGCE students spend in the university is devoted to subject-related work and that there has been a big reduction in generic theoretical elements in their courses. Such reductions were of course, in part involuntary response to increased demands on time made by the National Curriculum for ITT, backed by the force of frequent external inspection. However, they also resulted in part from reactions within ITT to the worst excesses of New Left ideological control and, more widely, from the same sort of dismissal of educational theory of any sort as abstract and irrelevant which helped to drive Conservative policies. This may explain the contrast between the bitter hostility expressed by UCET to the marginalisation of the disciplines of education and generic educational theory and its acceptance by many teacher educators.

David Lambert observed that the current model of ITT in London University Institute of Education had virtually discarded philosophy, history and sociology of education and 'all that jazz' and that, although the Institute is still an international centre of philosophy and sociology of education, PGCE students prefer the present balance in their courses. Indeed, he claimed, some would like even more concentration on the immediate requirements of classrooms and dislike the keynote lectures which are the residue of educational studies. He

---

154 Feiman-Nemser, F. *et al.* (1993). 'Are Mentor Teachers Teacher Educators?' in D. McIntyre, H. Hagger and M. Wilkin (eds). *Mentoring: Perspectives on School-Based Teacher Education.* London: Kogan Page.

considered the present courses to be highly sophisticated and rejected allegations that they are mere apprenticeship models or merely 'technicist' in character. Dr Lambert told me that in both primary and ITT subject lecturers had gained greater influence at the expense of lecturers in educational theory, but that there was little loss, since theoretical concerns of crucial importance arose naturally and sufficiently from courses in subject methods. In Warwick University School of Education, too, Richard Beare and Jim Campbell explained, there was by 1997 a much greater emphasis than in the past on courses in subject teaching and much less time available for more general educational studies. Lecturers at the University of Sunderland told me that there educational studies have been gradually reduced since 1982, so that now they had become of minor importance, with explicit theory surviving mainly in applied sociological forms of race, class and gender studies. They claimed that they had succeeded in basing broader pedagogical studies on specific subject courses, which they held to be much superior to what they were in the past.

John Furlong considered that the old Bristol University PGCE had been a poor professional preparation for teaching and that the quality of ITT, in terms of a practical performance approach, had much improved on that a decade ago, although he concedes that he made no public criticism of poor professional standards in ITT at the critical time. Now in the 'front-loaded' PGCE at Bristol systematic training is in place, with the emphasis on what to teach and how to teach it. Professor Furlong observed that the old disciplines of education had not only nearly disappeared from BEd and PGCE courses, but were much weaker than in the past in masters' courses in education. He would like to see more work in child development and curriculum theory, but not at the expense of the professionalism in teaching that has now been injected into ITT. He claimed that there are far fewer complaints from students about irrelevance and inefficiency in their courses than in the past.

David Reid maintained that theory should be used to explain past and present practice rather than to guide future practice. He opposed the use of predetermined theory to determine practice and held that general educational theory should arise from specific subject-related experience. However, he regretted that reductions in time devoted to theory entail that many students now have a poor understanding of historical and sociological influences on schooling, and thus find it difficult to grasp the rationale of current policies. He believed that many school mentors would prefer beginning teachers to have a firmer grasp of educational theory.

Lecturers at MMU's Didsbury Campus told me that its pedagogical courses were entirely subject-based. They were confident that subject tutors were fully capable of providing all the psychology, sociology and other kinds of education theory needed. Alan Goodwin believed that the teaching of separate 'education disciplines' outside the context of teaching a subject, as had been the norm 20–25 years ago, had been highly problematic. He was not hostile to the study of more general kinds of educational theory but considered these more appropriate for inservice study rather than ITT. He maintained that theoretical studies are exemplified at MMU in the context of subject teaching, classroom organisation and wider school issues as far as possible. He claimed this was the only viable solution, given that PGCE students spend only 12 weeks in university-based course. He conceded, however, that several of his MMU colleagues in what had been the Crewe College of Education defended courses in education disciplines as necessary to develop coherent thinking about education and fear that some key issues may not arise satisfactorily from even the best curriculum courses.

Some lecturers who generally welcomed the overall results of Conservative changes feared there may also have been some levelling down as well, with fewer inspirational young teachers, and a tendency to 'plateau' early on teaching practice, in the sense of regarding competency as a sufficient objective and not only as the basis for further development. Too many student teachers seemed to some of them to be concerned solely with means, not ends, and to adopt a narrowly instrumental view: 'If we are not teaching, do we need to be there?' Jerry Norton considered that secondary beginners were on average better prepared for teaching than their predecessors, as were primary teachers in maths, language and science, but he feared some breadth and flexibility have been lost in the process, so that beginning teachers may now be somewhat less reflective than before.

The main defenders of a more extensive place for educational theory in ITT come mainly from two clusters of educational ideas very much in dispute on most substantive issues: liberal educators and radical reconstructionists. They share a dislike for what is often termed 'technicism', the reduction of educational understanding to the sorts of competencies considered above, a process which, they allege, reduces teachers from professionals to technicians. David Carr has expressed concern that educational theory is often seen only as a way of providing a scientific, or quasi-scientific, basis for a particular sort of practice, rather than as an exploration of competing values and purposes. This position does not, of course, reject requirements of competencies out of hand, but emphasises the distinction between necessary and sufficient conditions for preparing beginning teachers in a satisfactory way. David Carr readily concedes that the conception of a liberal teacher education he advocates was often realised very inadequately in pre-1980s practice, but his articles offer a reasoned defence for seeking to hold on to its central concerns.[155] Of the teacher educators I met in 1997 the radical-reconstructionist case for a central role for educational studies in ITT was made most powerfully by Len Barton and Peter Gilroy.

Thus there was among my 1997 informants wide disagreement about the relationship between theory and practice in ITT and the significance and relevance of different types of educational theories and ideas. For those of us who accept the contestability of educational ideas this is to be expected and is not in itself any cause for concern. What is worth additional emphasis, however, is that I found that most of my informants considered that, since the Conservative reforms in ITT had begun, their own courses were better organised and more effective than in the past and that the new partnerships between the schools and teacher educators was superior to that before 1979.

---

155 See Carr, D. (1992). 'Practical Inquiry, Values and the Problem of Educational Theory' in *Oxford Review of Education*, 18 (3), pp. 241–51; (1993). 'Questions of Competence' in *British Journal of Educational Studies*, XXXXI (3), pp. 253–72; (1994). 'Educational Inquiry and Professional Knowledge: Towards a Copernican Revolution' in *Educational Studies*, 20 (1), pp. 33–52.

5 | SCITT

Not many schools opted to take part in SCITT, which represented a very radical departure from the old HEI-centred ITT. However, Andrew Hannan of the University of Plymouth considered it 'important to find out about those schools which do favour a radical shift away from HEI-based teacher education', since 'these schools may represent a growing trend or even a potentially divisive force which may be exploited to bring about the sort of radical shift the government appears to favour. They may alert us to basic problems with the status quo which need to be addressed even if we don't accept the government's proposals'.[156] In responses to a 1993 survey Hannan found that 71.6 per cent of 433 head teachers, 77.3 per cent of 267 parents, 71.4 per cent of 242 teacher education students, and even 62.5 per cent of 50 teacher education tutors were in favour of increasing the period of time student teachers spend in schools, by the amounts proposed which had recently been proposed by the DfE. The study also found that 63.7 per cent of head teachers and 57.1 per cent of tutors responding favoured moves to establish partnerships in ITT in which schools would play a more significant role than in the past, although only 26.5 per cent of tutors, as against 61.8 per cent of head teachers, favoured a transfer of resources to schools in reflect such a change in the balance of partnership.[157] Only 15.6 per cent of head teachers favoured the idea of schools being given the opportunity to set up training schemes which did not necessarily involve a teacher education institution at all, but Conservative ministers never suggested making such a path into teaching the norm, let alone compulsory.

---

156 Hannan, A. (1995). 'The Case for School-led Primary Teacher Training' in *Journal of Education for Teaching,* 21 (1), p. 25.
157 Hannan, 1995, p. 27.

A report on SCITT was issued by OFSTED in 1995. Six secondary consortia had been formed by then, with a total roll of 150 student teachers. Five worked with an HEI which validated a PGCE at the end of the course; only one operated entirely independently with QTS the sole award for its student teachers. OFSTED suggested that comparisons between the SCITT students and those in established HEI courses should be treated with 'considerable caution'.[158] OFSTED judged the quality of teacher training good in one consortium, satisfactory in three, but unsatisfactory in two, which in the following year improved to satisfactory grading. These initial results might well have been taken to indicate that SCITT was a worthwhile initiative which deserved to be continued, but that it would be extremely unwise to contemplate school-based ITT as the sole or main mode of entry into teaching.

SCITT student teachers must inevitably have access to fewer resources, including library facilities and course materials, compared with students in HEIs. Even with extra funding that gap is likely to remain significant. Although being part of a consortium helps mentors and other teachers in SCITT schools to link their own teaching situations with wider curricular and pedagogic concerns, explaining those links to student teachers is not their prime professional concern and it seems inevitable that HEIs will continue to have a significant advantage. If HEIs have been even minimally competent in past recruitment of subject specialists, then these ought to be better at explaining curricular and pedagogic matters than their former colleagues. In addition HEI staff have the advantage of being able to visit far more classrooms and thus of comparing and contrasting a larger range of teaching strategies.

If some understanding of the academic disciplines of education or generic educational theory is valuable in ITT, then support must be given to ensuring that HEI courses continue to be available, since such knowledge is undoubtedly better secured in them than through SCITT. At least this would be so, if in teaching practice HEIs did not use their own staff almost entirely for general liaison work with schools, rather than in observing and advising on their own specialist curriculum

---

158 OFSTED (1995). *School-centred Initial Teacher Training (1993–1994)*. HMSO, p. 3.

subjects. There is little reason to suppose that, say, a mathematics lecturer can assess a secondary school geography lesson better than the school's geography staff, or judge most of the work of a typical primary classroom as well as the regular class teacher.

The case against university-based ITT has been argued powerfully by the American scholar Martin Haberman, who claimed that it 'occurs in contexts which are divorced from the real world', In his analysis less than one in a hundred university education department dissertation topics would affect the work of classroom teachers. He found that:

> The typical pattern is for an ambitious individual who is good at 'graduate school' to endure a very few years of classroom teaching – which may have been good or bad teaching – go through a doctoral program comprised of courses and requirements which are irrelevant to the practice of teachers in classrooms, complete a dissertation irrelevant to practice, and then become an Assistant Professor of Education training future teachers.[159]

Haberman proposed five principles of excellence which should define the expertise of faculty in programmes of teacher education:

- The majority of teacher education faculty should be experienced, currently practising classroom teachers who have been identified as effective.

- Teacher educators are practitioners whose scholarship derives primarily from an experiential knowledge base of what works in classrooms in the real world.

- Teacher educators are expert teachers of low-income, minority and culturally diverse constituencies in need of the best teachers.

- Teacher educators are capable of coaching candidates' actual teaching behaviours and of modelling best practices for them.

---

159 Haberman, M. (1991). *The Dimensions of Excellence in Programs of Teacher Education*. Melbourne: IPA Education Policy Unit: Study Paper No. 26, p. 10.

- Teacher educators can prepare candidates for the non-teaching school-wide and community responsibilities of teachers in the real world.[160]

Not very many teacher educators in the United States met Haberman's requirements, and not many do here. He considered the basic proof of the inadequacy of ITT in the United States is that a very low proportion of education graduates go to teach in schools of greatest need and not many stay long if they do. Haberman expected in 1991 that shrinking state budgets and public dissatisfaction with undermanned schools would lead many states to make certification for college graduates voluntary and leave to those school districts the total responsibility for preparing their own teachers.[161]

Haberman claimed that there was 'substantial evidence from students [in university education programmes], recent graduates and experienced teachers of lack of substance and irrelevance' in their coursework.[162] He listed five principles of excellence which should shape ITT:

- Teacher education occurs on-site in a functioning school.

- Teachers-to-be learn to teach by functioning in the role of teacher and being held responsible for the full range of tasks and duties required of other practising teachers.

- Teaching is taught best by a process of coaching when the coaches are practising teachers released from classrooms to coach a few beginners on a full time basis.

- Teacher education programmes are enhanced and supplemented by workshops offered to meet beginning teachers' particular needs.

- Traditional university courses may be of some use to teachers after they have had a few years of teaching practice and have developed the experiential knowledge base for evaluating what is being offered.

For several years school boards in tough American city areas have had to resort to school-based training for underqualified or

---

160 Haberman, 1991, p. 12.
161 Haberman, 1991, pp. 32–3.
162 Haberman, 1991, p. 21.

unqualified teachers, because not enough of the large annual output of college and university graduates in education will teach in those schools. As a result many boards have taken similar initiatives to those in Britain to organise and legitimise this alternative method of entering teaching.

The proof of the pudding must be in the eating. If school-based systems display the narrow limitations anticipated by some critics, they are unlikely to last long, provided that intending teachers have a choice between school-based and tertiary-based teacher preparation, and that employers of teachers can choose from products of both. What is more likely is that the very existence of SCITT, even if confined to only a small number of clusters of schools, will act as a competitive spur to HEIs which offer ITT. Overall, the balance of educational advantage may prove to be with tertiary-based, rather than school-based, entry into teaching, but adequate and fair financial arrangements should be available to ensure that potential teachers and schools who wish to go along the SCITT path should also be able to do so.

6 | Ideological Capture

Although the amount of time available for educational theory of any kind was much less in 1997 than 1979, I found that New Left proselytising was as intense as ever in some of the remaining areas in which it could be practised. Nothing could be less true than that Conservative governments had carried out an ideological purge of their own during their years of office. New Left ideological zeal flourished most of all in ubiquitous courses claiming to counter sexism and racism or to promote equal opportunities, but it also powerfully influenced many of the curriculum courses which had survived the attenuation of the disciplines of education and generic educational studies. Curriculum courses in science and mathematics, reading and literacy, were as likely to show the signs of New Left hegemony as were history or social studies.

Race and gender

Stephen Ball has observed that during the 1980 some neo-Marxists 'reinvented themselves as feminists or anti-racists' and turned from 'class analysis' as 'the primary variable', with 'race, gender and, later, disability and sexual orientation coming to the fore both in analytical perspectives and in a new but tentative liaison between theory and practice.'[163] Indoctrination is easier in anti-racism and anti-sexism courses than in the educational disciplines, in which it is difficult, although not impossible, of course, to prevent students from becoming aware that there are respectable alternatives to the convictions of their lecturers. As John Wilson of Oxford University had noted, lecturers in topics involving race, gender and special needs did not require scholarly credentials; the lecturers only needed to 'present themselves for the most part as leaders of the faithful:

---

163 Ball, 1995, p. 258.

co-workers in areas where, it is believed, the proper ideology is already clear and students only need to be initiated, informed and inspired'. A 'desire to have identifiable enemies which need to be directly combated' in 'a series of crusades' readily displaced any pretence of objective study.[164]

Accusations of racism and sexism became more and more rife during the 1980s, although they did little to explain why white boys from working-class families were so conspicuous among 'disadvantaged' groups. Moving into anti-racism did not, of course, require any abjuration of neo-Marxist doctrines. Mairtin Mac an Ghaill of the University of Sheffield School of Education, for example, became an authority on 'schooling masculinities' or how 'schooling processes can be seen to form gendered identities, marking out "correct" or "appropriate" styles of being'.[165] He argued that in the past schools confirmed these identities, because they had 'the power to define what is normal and "ordinary" male behaviour', but his mission was to overthrow stereotypes of males as 'powerful and authoritative' and to disrupt 'male group networks' which are 'one of the most oppressive arenas for the production and regulation of masculinities'.[166] Outside the area of opposing sexism, he admitted to 'the apparent failure of progressive schooling to create a more egalitarian society' but considered failure resulted from lukewarm pursuit of the project and he still held that 'comprehensive reorganisation, child-centred pedagogy, anti-racism and anti-sexism are key

---

164 Wilson, J. (1989). 'Topics, Ideology and Discipline in Teacher Education' in *Educational Review*, 41 (1), p. 33.
165 Haywood, C. and Mac an Ghaill, M. (1996). 'Schooling masculinities' in M. Mac an Ghaill (ed). *Understanding Masculinities*. London: Open University Press, p. 50. The Open University was a prolific source of neo-Marxist publications. Many Open University courses, such as its 1981 E353 *State, Education and Society*, were compiled almost entirely by neo-Marxists. Open University publications were used widely in neo-Marxist courses in ITT. One book, *Schools on Trial*, written in 1985 by Colin Fletcher, Maxine Caron and Wyn Williams, defended four 'democratic comprehensives' which had justly been severely criticised by angry parents, and even by Left-wing LEAs and HMI generally sympathetic to progressivist innovations. One of the schools Risinghill (Raising Hell) in North London was closed, or at least merged with a neighbouring school. Its head teacher became a teacher educator! Penguin Education vied with the Open University Press as the most influential propagator of New Left educational ideology, but at least it received no public funding.
166 Haywood and Mac an Ghaill, 1996, p. 54.

elements of the modernist project, informed by a belief in collectivism, humanism, rational progression and social justice'.[167]

Bias and one-sidedness were rampant in some courses concerned with race and gender, whose outlines or reading lists I saw in 1997. MMU's Didsbury College provided some of the worst examples. Its 'Professional Issues Resource Book' defined 'sexism' as a term 'generally used to refer to the prejudices and discrimination faced by girls and women'.[168] From its reading list 'invariably' could be substituted for 'generally' in that stipulative definition. Students were assured, with reference to 'Stanworth, *Gender and Schooling*, Hutchinson, 1981', that 'there is evidence that girls see themselves as academic under-achievers',[169] despite very ample evidence on the contrary that the average academic achievement of females at virtually every age-level, but especially in the early years of education, is significantly higher than that of males. Among the 'sexist assumptions' disadvantaging females which MMU students were still warned against in 1997 were mistaken 'attitudes to the use of Ms'.[170]

The MMU Resources Book claimed that discrimination is routinely practised 'for the benefit of those who control the process – normally white, middle-class men' on grounds of 'race, culture, class, disability, age and sexual orientation as well as gender'. The term 'race' was dismissed as 'inaccurate', but was also extensively used by MMU itself in claims such as that race is 'associated with a wide range of demeaning stereotypes of non-white people'.[171] Because of white prejudice, it alleged, 'the beliefs and practices that make up non-white cultures are very often the trigger-points for racism', and in the United Kingdom 'many non-white immigrants' had 'low class status and therefore suffered double discrimination. Their struggle for basic human rights often brings them into conflict with working-class white citizens who have also been deprived of their rights.

---

[167] Mac an Ghaill, M. (1996). 'Sociology of Education, State Schooling and Social Class: Beyond Critiques of the New Right Hegemony' in *British Journal of Sociology of Education,* 17 (2), p. 167.
[168] Manchester Metropolitan University Faculty of Community Studies, Law and Education (1997). *Secondary Programme of School-Based Initial Teacher Training: Professional Issues Resources Book*, p. 20.
[169] MMU, 1997, p. 22
[170] MMU, 1997, p. 23
[171] MMU, 1997, p. 21.

The widening gap between rich and poor makes the latter a growing group'.[172]

MMU claimed that in Britain West Indian children are deliberately 'placed disproportionately in lower streams' of schools, and 'often in relation to their supposed behaviour than their academic performance', since 'it is anticipated that they will be noisy and argumentative'. On the other hand it claimed that Asian children, especially girls, are deliberately disadvantaged by being led to believe that 'being quiet and passive earns approval'.[173] Since the teachers apparently exert such vast psychological power, it seems a pity a few do not try to persuade some West Indian boys to be a little more quiet in classrooms or urge Asian girls to be more noisy and argumentative.

The reading lists at MMU recommended mainly works written from the one perspective and often lacked even a single source to challenge their arguments, but this is not unusual among those who claim to foster reflection and critical thought.[174] Many other MMU courses also concern themselves with race and gender issues. The *Subject Handbook for History*, for example, avers that 'in particular trainees need to be encouraged to build into schemes of work and lesson plans multicultural and gender elements as they relate to an understanding of history'. The HE tutor 'needs to ensure that trainees are aware of the equal opportunities requirements of the National Curriculum and/or the importance and significance of equal opportunities to the secondary curriculum' and to 'discuss how

---

172 MMU, 1997, p. 22.
173 MMU, 1997. p. 24.
174 Many lengthy denunciations by teacher educators of Conservative policy and 'New Right' thinking fail to provide a direct reference to even a single article or book written by those they denounce. Examples include Jonathan, R. (1990). 'State Education Service or Prisoner's Dilemma: The "Hidden Hand" as Source of Education Policy' in *British Journal of Educational Studies*, XXXVIII (2), pp. 116–32; Saunders, M. and Halpin, D. (1990). The TVEI and the National Curriculum: A Cautionary Note' in *British Journal of Educational Studies*, XXXVIII (3), pp. 224–36; Mac an Ghaill, M. (1996). 'Sociology of Education, State Schooling and Social Class: Beyond Critiques of the New Right Hegemony' in *British Journal of Sociology of Education*, 17 (2), pp. 163–76; Sidgwick, S., Mahoney, P. and Hextall, I. (1994). 'A Gap in the Market? A Consideration of Market Relations in Teacher Education' in *British Journal of Sociology of Education*, 15 (4), pp. 467–79.

the study of history can enhance pupils' understanding of equal opportunities with particular reference to cultural and gender issues. The subject mentor 'needs to indicate how the department responds to National Curriculum requirements on equal opportunities' and 'discuss ways the trainee's schemes of work could address, in particular, multicultural and gender education'. Finally the trainee 'needs to know and understand how the study of history can contribute to pupils' understanding of issues relating to equal opportunities, in particular, cultural and gender issues'.[175] The main content for teaching in this *Handbook for History* consists of 'Make (sic) Medieval Realms and Making of the UK', 'Multicultural History', 'Women and History Reviews', 'Local History and Fieldwork' and 'Teaching about the Holocaust'.

In addition at MMU, 'On the matter of equal opportunities, advice may be sought using the following telephone contacts …': the numbers of 'Ethnic Minorities', 'Lesbians in Education' and 'Manchester Gay Centre' follow.[176] If MMU students fully adopt the standpoint so constantly thrust upon them, it would hardly be surprising if difficulties arose on occasion in their schools. The MMU *Course Handbook for the Three Year Course Leading to BEd* offers advice on 'Claims about your Equal Opportunities Teaching by pupils or parents', since 'Such complaints challenge the credibility of your teaching, and you must make a response, explaining the value of what you are doing'. Advice is also offered on how to deal with regular staff or ancillary staff who make 'racist or sexist comments'. Reports should be made to the class/subject teacher or mentor, and if the offender be one of these, a higher authority must be informed. Given the loose definitions of racism and sexism in MMU, and the frank speech of Lancashire cleaners and caretakers, and not only white ones, tense situations must frequently arise.

Appendix A contains a few examples of one-sided reading lists on topics in ITT relating to race and/or gender. Had they

---

175 Manchester Metropolitan University Faculty of Community Studies, Law and Education: Didsbury School of Education in partnership with schools and colleges (1997). *Subject Handbook for History*, pp. 84–5.
176 Manchester Metropolitan University Faculty of Community Studies, Law and Education: Didsbury School of Education in partnership with schools and colleges (1997). *PGCE Secondary One Year Course: 1997–8 Course Handbook,* p. 89.

no personal or other independent experience, students might well be led to believe from such utterly unbalanced reading lists that the central problem in education is how to save females and non-whites from oppression. Notes issued to PGCE students at London University Institute of Education to accompany the 1996 keynote lecture included a paper by Gerald Grace entitled 'Overcoming prejudice and discrimination as barriers to equal opportunities in education'. His inability to find 'explicit and visible' discrimination in any British educational law did not discourage Professor Grace, who alleged that discrimination continued to lurk in 'the implicit, covert and "unintentional" mode'. He considered that 'there does seem little doubt that it exists in institutions and in society', although not, of course, in his own institution.

In the reading lists cited, most of the works on gender devote much time to explaining why females 'under perform' in education. Rob Moore of Homerton College, Cambridge, has summed up the factors anti-sexism courses adduce to explain why females and non-whites are discriminated against educationally as follows:

- the gender and racial bias of school texts ...
- androcentric and ethnocentric language
- sexist and racist teacher stereotypes, expectations and treatment of pupils
- aspects of school organisation
- the domination of school staffs by white males ...
- the failure of teachers to check sexist and racist behaviour
- the imposition of traditional relationships and hierarchies through education policy
- resistance to developing school equal opportunities policies and 'good practice'.[177]

There is thus a formidable range of possible explanations for the relative failure of females in British education, the only

---

177 Moore, R. (1996). 'Back to the Future: the Problem of Change and the Possibilities of Advance in the Sociology of Education' in *British Journal of Sociology of Education*, 17 (3), p. 149.

problem being that there is no such relative failure. Instead, females enjoy greater educational success than males. Even when race and gender are combined, it is found that, family income and the like allowed for, Asian girls considerably outperform white boys. The non-existence of the problem does not, however, prevent huge amounts of money and time being devoted to its solution, but at the same time the real problem of significant educational underachievement by boys remains largely ignored.

Some other ITT courses

What follows here is necessarily impressionistic, even bitty, and may be unrepresentative, although all the courses to which I refer were brought to my attention during or after my interviews by teacher educators who did not seem to think any of their institutions' offerings worthy of special censure or praise in respect of the fairness of their treatment of contestable matters. It would take considerable space to demonstrate the imbalances and bias in the courses and reading lists mentioned here, but interested readers are urged to pick just one or two lists and sample their recommendations or requirements.

A topic entitled *English: 1E136: Judgement and Analysis: Canon Formation and the Making of Culture* is available in Manchester University's BAQTS course. It deals with '... the main themes of historical development to which current British society is heir and by which it was shaped: revolution (the rights of man and the rights of women); landscape and emotion; romanticism and the rise of childhood; the making of the English class system. The two works in its 'Introductory Reading' are Edward Said (1992) *Culture and Imperialism,* Chatto and Windus and Raymond Williams (1958) *Culture and Society 1780–1950,* Chatto and Windus.

In the University of Bristol PGCE Educational and Professional Studies File for 1997–98 three books constitute the 'Annotated Reading List' for 'Developing common purposes in schools', part of Strand D: 'Developing as a Professional'. Two are published by the Open University Press: Fullan, M. and Hargreaves, A. (1992). *What's Worth Fighting for in Your School: Working Together for Improvement,* and Whittaker, F. (1993). *Managing Change in Schools.* The third was Lawton, D. (1992). *Education and Politics in the 1990s: Conflict or Consensus?,* published by the Falmer Press.

Not many books about education of a general theoretical character appeared on reading lists I saw in 1997, but a few were selected frequently, such as John Holt's *How Children Fail* and his *Why Children Succeed* and the 1971 *Teaching as a Subversive Activity* of Postman and Weingarner, which claimed that for most children there was little relevance in learning to read, since they could always get what they needed from television, cinema and the like. It is a melancholy reflection on teacher education that this book was still a frequently recommended text in 1997, whereas Postman's subsequent recantation in his 1980 *Teaching as a Conserving Activity* appeared on no list I saw.[178] Warwick University opened a section called 'A question of thinking' in its *PGCE Secondary Courses 1997–1998: Core Programme Study Guide* with a quotation from the early unreconstructed Postman: 'All our knowledge results from questions, which is another way of saying that question-asking is our most important intellectual tool'. This is part of the 'readiness' dogma which has found great favour in ITT: children are only judged ready for an activity if and when they show an interest in it by asking questions about it. In reality, of course, a large number of children think of questions to ask after they

---

178 Postman, N. and Weingartner, C. (1971). *Teaching as a Subversive Activity*. London: Penguin Books. Postman, N (1980). *Teaching as a Conserving Activity*. New York: Dell. 'Ideological selectivity on the part of New Left educationists may also be ascertained by examining reading lists to see which works of James S. Coleman are cited. In his 1966 *Equality of Educational Opportunity*, published in Washington DC by the United States Government Printing Office, Coleman concluded that the policies of schools had very little influence on educational outcomes. A decade later a wiser Coleman reviewed his earlier findings which, as he increasingly realised, ran counter to experience, logic and intuition, and he therefore engaged in further empirical research. This is reported in *High School Achievement*, published in 1982 in New York by Basic Books and written by Coleman with the support of Thomas Hoffer and Sally Kilgore. This study identified several features of schools which strongly correlated with high levels of student achievement, after all background factors (income, class, ethnicity, etc.) were fully taken into account. The comparatively higher achieving schools demanded regular school attendance, set high standards of personal conduct, maintained strong and consistent discipline, offered a rigorous and demanding curriculum, assigned regular homework (in the case of secondary schools) and ensured that it was marked regularly and systematically monitored. I am confident that in ITT courses in Britain in 1999 it will be found that for every reference to Coleman's 1982 findings five will be found to the 1966 work he subsequently repudiated.'

have been introduced to an activity and learned its basic structure. This is the case in games and songs as well as in reading and arithmetic. 'Readiness' beliefs further widen the achievement gap between children from educationally supportive and unsupportive homes, since the former usually appear to their teachers to be much more ready to start learning whatever it may be.

It was rare to come across on any reading lists or course outlines the name of any writer who could in educational terms be described as 'New Right', 'Old Right', Conservative or Liberal, but some lists were fair and representative and deserve credit. At the University of Newcastle, Peter Fisher's readings for his Humanities course included Paul Hirst's *Liberal Education and the Nature of Knowledge* and a chapter from the Hirst and Peters *The Logic of Education*, together with two books by Peter Gordon and Douglas Holly's *Humanities in Adversity*. The London University Institute of Education's recommended reading list in its 1997–98 *Secondary PGCE Partnership in Training Handbook* included *Fifteen Thousand Hours, The Critical Dictionary of Educational Concepts*, edited by R. Barrow and G. Milburn, and L. A. Reid's *Ways of Understanding and Education*. That Louis Arnaud Reid was once a Professor of Education in the London Institute may have helped his appearance on this reading list, although his successors Paul Hirst and Richard Peters were absent.

When politically incorrect thinkers gained mention, it was rarely in any good light. In the University of Newcastle's unit on 'Mainstream School and Code of Practice', Lead Tutor Alan Millward began with, 'Cyril Burt, "the first educational psychologist" but not the first academic to doctor his data ...'[179] Millward's colleague, Liz Todd, Lead Tutor for 'Learning and Cognition 11–16', writing in praise of Vygotsky, claimed that before that sage enlightened the world 'the child has been seen as learning by conditioning (behaviourism) or as lone thinkers actively developing their own structures of thought (Piaget) or as processors of information, rather like an extremely complex computer (information processing theory)'.[180] This dismissive

---

179 University of Newcastle upon Tyne Department of Education. *PGCE Secondary Course 1997–8*, p. 35.
180 *op. cit.*, p. 31.

attitude to significant thinkers is among reasons why teacher education fell into some disrepute. Fortunately, 'the new perspective resulting from Vygotsky is that children are not lone thinkers acting on the world and developing their thinking'. The University of Newcastle 1997–98 History programme had as its only references under 'A framework for learning history' the names of Vygotsky and Jerome Bruner.

Teaching of reading became an area of ideological dispute as well as technical disagreements during the 1960s and has remained so, even though the connection between the New Left and the 'whole-language' approaches seems contingent and fortuitous. 'Whole-language' and 'look-and-say' advocates broadly hold that reading can effectively be taught by providing children with highly interesting material to read, without much need for drill in rules and patterns of language. Some hold that drills put children off reading and are thus not only of little value but actually harmful, but after extensive international debate the balance of argument lies with those who urge the inclusion of a powerful phonic component in the teaching of reading. Adams and Bruck concluded after an exhaustive review of relevant research:

> Whenever children who cannot discover the alphabetic principle independently are denied explicit instruction on the regularities and conventions of the letter strings, reading-disability may well be the eventual consequence.[181]

Most children starting school can discriminate phonemes (i.e. individual speech sounds), but rapid progress with reading requires the further ability to manipulate them in thought and speech, which many children acquire only if given phonic drills, although word recognition methods are also of considerable value and should be incorporated into reading schemes.

There seemed in 1997 to be a much better balance in courses in teaching reading than before the introduction of the National Curriculum. Course outlines which filled me with confidence included those of the University of Warwick Institute of Education Primary PGCE for 'Reading' and 'Spelling and Handwriting'

---

181 Adams, M. J. and Bruck, M. (1993). 'Word Recognition: The Interface of Educational Policies and Scientific Research' in *Reading and Writing: An Interdisciplinary Journal,* p. 131.

and the MMU English PGCE Primary Programme. *The School-Based Work Handbook* for the University of Exeter PGCE Primary provided exercises which are a very useful introduction to understanding the reading behaviour of children, although suggested readings on actual teaching methods seemed one-sided and failed to do justice to phonic-based approaches. Some reading lists, such as the University of Southampton's 'Pre-Reading' for 'Language and Communication' in its PGCE course, were outdated and did not include the Kingman Report or any responses to it. Indeed, that reading list was not only outdated but would have been indefensibly unbalanced at any time:

> Barnes, D. et al. (1986). *Language, the Learner and the School*. 3rd edn. Penguin and Heinemann Education.
> Beard, R. (1977). *Use of Language: A Common Approach*. SCAA.
> Beard, R. (1993). *Teaching Literacy: Balancing Perspectives*. Hodder and Stoughton.
> Britton, J. et al. (1976). *Language as Educator*. Ward Lock.
> Bullock Report: *A Language for Life*. (1975). HMSO.
> Flanders, N. (1970). *Analysing Teacher Behaviour*. Addison-Wesley.
> Holt, J. (1969). *How Children Fail*. Penguin.
> Marland, M. (1977). *Language Across the Curriculum*. Heinemann.
> National Association for the Teaching of English (1976). *Language Across the Curriculum: Guidelines for Schools*. NATE in conjunction with Ward Lock.
> Postman, N. and Weingartner, C. (1971). *Teaching as a Subversive Activity*. Penguin.

Some suggestions should appear on any such list, such as the 1975 Bullock Report in its time, although in 1997 one might think it more appropriate to cite the Kingman Report which covered similar ground two decades later. Barnes, Beard, Britton and Marland are all respectable proponents of the case for what was in its time 'New English', with its dislike for formal language studies and its emphasis on student experience, but some voices on the other side should also be presented. Flanders' work on classroom interaction is still of interest, but does not deal specifically with language. The Holt and the Postman and Weingartner books, in so far as they are helpful at all, especially need to be balanced by authors who favour structured learning.

By 1997 many science courses in ITT had been subjected to ideological take-over by radical constructivism. Constructivism in science education began with an interest in 'student misconceptions'.[182] This was valid, since understanding of how and why children, or adults, get things wrong is very helpful in enabling them to get them right. However, children's misconceptions were elevated by radical constructionists to the status of 'children's science', to which they accorded a significance comparable with that of any other sort of science. Rosalind Driver and her colleagues claimed that 'the way in which science ideas are constructed by pupils reflects the nature and status of science as public knowledge' and constitutes a valid 'alternative conception' of science.[183]

Although every sensible teacher will make appropriate use of the experiences children bring with them to school, very often there is no direct line from commonsense understanding based on personal experience to scientific understanding. Many features of our everyday experience, such as colour, are of little relevance in scientific explanation. 'Natural' differences between substances such as wood, coal, iron, silver, oil, water, etc. are central to ordinary observation and experience, but have very limited explanatory power in chemistry. Many of the basic concepts of modern science, such as atoms, hydrogen, neutrons, genes, DNA, are simply outside the realm of everyday perception. Were this not so, every people would have advanced to scientific understanding, since all have considerable everyday knowledge of the natural phenomena around them. Contrary to constructivist claims, learning a subject, or an area of experience, requires the initiation of the learner into a set of rules or principles, accompanied by appropriate techniques, developed in a publicly shared tradition. It is not necessary, or even remotely possible, for the learner to re-invent the wheel and the whole of human knowledge.

The radical constructivists' elevation of the value of children's misunderstandings was accompanied by the rejection of the possibility of securing objective knowledge common among neo-Marxists and their numerous allies in relativist and

---

[182] Driver, R. and Easley, J. (1978). 'Pupils and Paradigms: A Review of Literature Related to Concept Development in Adolescent Science Students' in *Studies in Science Education*, 5, pp. 61–84.
[183] Driver, R., Squires, A., Rushworth, P. and Woods-Robinson, V. (1994). *Making Sense of Secondary Science*. London: Routledge, p. 7 (cited in Matthews, 1995, p. 216).

subjectivist epistemology. This rejection must, of course, transform the role of the teacher. Driver defined 'the core commitment of a constructivist position' as 'that knowledge is not transmitted directly from one knower to another, but is actively built up by the learner'.[184] She also claimed that 'Although we may assume the existence of an external world we do not have direct access to it; science as public knowledge is not so much a discovery as a carefully checked construction'.[185] And one which all children must construct for themselves! The radical constructivists elevated such half truths to the whole truth in the same way that neo-Marxist sociologists such as Michael F. D. Young held that knowledge was not merely socially constructed in the sense that it depends on public means of validation, but *only* socially constructed in the sense of being entirely a creation of ideology or power.

Instead of being merely a bizarre aberration, radical constructivism rapidly became orthodoxy in ITT during the 1980s. David Hartley of the Institute for Education and Lifelong Learning, University of Dundee, noted

> ... within teacher education, constructivist pedagogy was applied by academics to those very trainee teachers who might themselves come to apply it later in the school, albeit within the confines of the National Curriculum ... leaving a curious mix: a curriculum of competence and a pedagogy of constructivism.[186]

In a review in the same journal number in which Hartley's article appeared, Tom Bryce of the Faculty of Education, University of Strathclyde, started with the claim that 'Books on constructivist approaches to learning and teaching are to be welcomed'. On that basis he has had much to welcome in recent years. Bryce added that 'there is a tendency to ascribe everything good and effective in teaching to constructivism'.[187] Indeed, by 1990 the University of Leeds, a leading centre of radical

---

[184] Driver *et al.*, 1994, p. 5.
[185] Driver, R. and Oldham, V. (1986). 'A Constructivist Approach to Curriculum Development in Science' in *Studies in Science Education,* 13, p. 109.
[186] Hartley, D. (1998). 'Repeat Prescription: the National Curriculum for Initial Teacher Training' in *British Journal of Educational Studies*, 46 (1), p. 70.
[187] Bryce, T. (1998). Review of Catherine Twomey Fornot in *British Journal of Educational Studies*, 46 (1), p. 84.

constructivist science teaching, was able to produce a bibliography of constructivist research listing over 1,000 works.[188]

The only reading lists for ITT courses in science education in which I noted in 1997 any references critical of radical constructivism were in Sheffield Hallam University, King's College, University of London, and Warwick University, although there must be several I did not have the opportunity to see. One would hope that proponents of critical and reflective thought, as radical constructivists claim to be, would at least confront their students with arguments such as Strike's against epistemological relativism:

> If every idea is as good as every other, and if that which certifies an idea for a particular student is the fact that it is a personal construct, it is simply mysterious as to why we should teach or why students should care what we teach.[189]

Intending teachers of science might also reflect with profit on Paul Hirst's argument that

> ... it is a necessary feature of knowledge as such that there be public criteria whereby the true is distinguishable from the false, the good from the bad, the right from the wrong. It is the existence of these criteria which gives objectivity to knowledge.[190]

The results of a decade and more of constructivism in science have been poor in all the English-speaking countries providing evidence. Paul Black and Arthur Lucas of King's College, University of London, commented that in the United Kingdom the 'extent to which the recent work on children's intuitive ideas about the natural world has paid off in terms of improved classroom practice is so far disappointing'.[191] Joan Bliss and other lecturers in that same institution have noted wisely that 'to imagine that socially constructed knowledge in areas like

---

188 Carmichael, P. et al. (1990). *Research on Students' Conceptions in Science: A Bibliography*. Leeds: University of Leeds, Children's Learning in Science Project.
189 Strike, K. (1987). 'Towards a Coherent Constructivism' in J. D. Novak (ed). *Misconceptions and Educational Strategies*. Cornell University Education Department, vol. 1, p. 489.
190 Hirst, P. (1974). 'Liberal Education and the Nature of Knowledge' in his *Knowledge and the Curriculum*. London: Routledge, p. 43.
191 Black, P. and Lucas, A. (eds) (1993). *Children's Informal Ideas in Science*. New York: Routledge, p. 190.

science, technology and mathematics is everyday knowledge is to misunderstand the purpose of schooling, which is the pupil's initiation into grappling with the theoretical aspects of these domains'.[192]

Perhaps the oddest aspect of radical constructivism is the way in which, first, an epistemology which has a purely contingent relationship to political ideologies, and, secondly, a pedagogy even more contingent to politics, can become the object of ideological attachment and dogmatic defence. This case is in its way especially puzzling, since classical Marxism was so firmly attached to dialectical materialism and a rigidly realist epistemology. But similar reversals have taken place in matters which can more obviously become politicised, such as the relative power of heredity and environment on human thought and action. Political correctness currently holds that some important characteristics, such as homosexuality or, in Australia, 'Aboriginality', are purely a matter of genes, whereas others, such as intelligence, are determined by environment and experience.

The failure of many teacher educators to provide a fair range of readings and sources for their students seems to provide *prima facie* evidence that ideological capture continues to be a problem in HEIs concerned with teacher education, despite claims of draconian censorship from the Right. A notable feature of the HEIs whose staff offer even the most atrociously biased courses is that elaborate institutional apparatuses exist in them for the stated purpose of establishing some sort of 'quality control'. These committees may grab the occasional organisational gnat, as when it is noted that the summation of marks allocated for separate units in a course may total more than 100 per cent, but ideological camels are swallowed without difficulty.

Teacher educators and research

Although Conservative governments, through OFSTED and the TTA, significantly reduced the amount of time devoted in ITT to educational theory, their insistence that engagement in educational research should form part of their professional duties has forced many teacher educators to attend to theoretical concerns much more than in the past. Another presumably unintended effect of this research requirement has been to

---

192 Bliss, J., Askew, M. and Macrae, S. (1996). 'Effective Teaching and Learning: Scaffolding Revisited' in *Oxford Review of Education*, 22 (1), pp. 59–60.

counteract the shift of power within teacher education from former university to old college lecturers, since a far higher proportion of the former have successfully engaged in research and been published outside the walls of the particular HEI. It is therefore not surprising that critics of the research requirement come mainly from former college staff, although the correlation is far from perfect. At the University of Plymouth Ken Lawson explained to me why he was opposed to compulsory research. He saw himself as a teacher concerned with actual practice, not as a researcher, and feared that unproductive research might prove a diversion from better uses of his time. Mike Harrison also expressed dislike of research requirements when these are not related to function. Sceptics such as David Leat and Rod Bramald, who have themselves a solid research record, argued that research interests distract some teacher educators from their teaching role; some good teacher educators carry out little or no significant original research and are unlikely ever to do so. This observation raises a useful caution. It is a worthwhile attribute to be able to carry out independent research, but there is little reason to think that all forms of research have great potentiality for enhancing the work of all teacher educators. There are good grounds for supposing that a wider knowledge of educational thought might more often be more appropriate than immersion in narrowly focused empirical research. A major weakness in many higher degree studies in teacher education is that frequently they build on too narrow a foundation. But the research requirement undermines allegations that the Conservatives sought to 'dumb down' the teacher educators.

Much of the research activity carried out by teacher educators to meet these new conditions of employment never results even in a paper given to colleagues within a HEI, let alone sees the light in any published form. Articles based on educational research which are published in educational journals demonstrate very clearly the continued ascendancy of the New Left. The same is true of papers presented to conferences of teacher educators. Rosie Turner-Bisset of the University of Hertfordshire provided the following as an example of what she held to be exemplary teaching of history in the primary classroom:

> A teacher stands up in front of her class of Year 5 children. She is wearing a cloth cap, an old overcoat and boots. She talks directly to

the class in role as an unemployed cotton worker, taking part in one of the hunger marches of the twenties and thirties ... This teacher believes that history is an enquiry-based discipline, which involves both interpretation of evidence and imaginative construction of the past ... The story she has written is fictional, but based on fact ... If the children only know about the Jarrow march, they might believe that they were the only people who marched, that they were all well-fed and well looked after ... The teacher has a lively class of 28 Year 5 children, 2 of whom are statemented. She has a part-time assistant to help her with these children. They have a shortish attention span ... The statemented children and others with reading difficulties will have access to the material through the story and acting ... The teacher knows that she is happy to stand in front of her class dressed oddly, and act out a role ... She sees herself as a descendant, albeit a comfortably-off middle-class descendant of the working people who helped to make the mill-owners wealthy ... she regards it as an important end that they [the pupils] are able to be critical of texts of all kinds, of evidence, of media representation and of political propaganda ... She has secondary purposes in this lesson, to address issues of community and citizenship, and moral issues to do with the right to work ...[193]

Of course, many teachers are would-be politicians and/or actors, and this teacher would perhaps be even happier starring in agitprop such as *Brassed Off* or *An Inspector Calls*, but it is remarkable that a teacher educator should so openly endorse indoctrination and call it encouragement to critical thinking.

A striking feature of many New Left educational theorists is that the more indoctrinative they are, the more do they proclaim their attachment to 'critical' and 'reflective' thinking. 'Critical' and 'reflective' theory are branches of the wider ideological phenomenon of postmodernism and deconstructionism, from which many New Left educationists had sought solace and comfort. By 1997 the adjectives 'critical' and 'reflective', when used about teaching, were often indicators of uncritical and unreflective New Left activism and as far from their ordinary language meaning as 'democratic' or 'people's' when used in

---

[193] Turner-Bisset, R. (1997). *The Knowledge Bases of the Expert Teacher*. Paper presented at the British Educational Research Association Annual Conference, York University, pp. 7–10.

the titles of states. Kathy Hall of Leeds Metropolitan University wrote in a review of a book by David Hartley, himself a critical thinker in this particular sense,

> However, I take hope from the work of McLaren and Giroux and other critical theorists who argue for a critical pedagogy explicitly geared to a more just and democratic society. At a minimum, one must take some solace, as Hartley does, from the likelihood that learner-centred pedagogy, while functional for some post-Fordist work regimes, nevertheless encourages a questioning and reflective attitude in the learner and one which could lead to the construction of counter-discourses.[194]

Of course, Blair's Britain is for Kathy Hall little, if at all, more just and democratic than the wicked world of Thatcher and Major. She discreetly failed to name any societies which meet her ideals, but I would suspect that those she favours are not very favourable to the construction of counter-discourses. In an article boldly entitled 'Critical Social Research and the Academy: the Role of Organic Intellectuals in Educational Research', Iram Siraj-Blatchford roundly asserted that 'all research is inevitably politically committed'.[195] Siraj-Blatchford's own research was, indeed, obviously politically committed: to a version of neo-Marxism in which Gramsci's concept of an organic intellectual is misinterpreted as endorsement of the impossibility of disinterested study.

It would be unfair to cite only minnows who lurk in the neo-Marxist theoretical pool. Let us consider one or two of the pikes, such as Wilfred Carr of Sheffield University School of Education and Stephen Kemmis, formerly of the School of Education of the University of East Anglia and now a professor in an Australian university. Carr and Kemmis expounded their notion of 'action research' as follows:

> action research rejects the positivist notions of rationality, objectivity, and truth ... For the action researcher, the end is the

---

194 Hall, K. (1998). Review of David Hartley in *British Journal of Educational Studies*, 46 (3), p. 339.
195 Siraj-Blatchford, I. (1995). 'Critical Social Research and the Academy: the Role of Organic Intellectuals in Educational Research' in *British Journal of Sociology of Education*, 15 (1), p. 209.

improvement of practice; for the positivist researcher, the end is theoretical completeness and practical application of findings ... The action researcher sees the relationship between theory and practice as dialectical, with both being developed in the historical process of research and action; the positivist researcher treats theory and practice ahistorically, as if correct theories and correct action could be defined universally.

The interests of action research are not in the development of abstract theoretical languages communicating universal truths, nor in scepticism, proclaiming universal uncertainty. Rather its interest is in developing a theoretical position grounded in the real life of social practice on the one hand and a critical theory of society on the other.

This kind of action research may be described as 'emancipatory' because the group itself takes responsibility for its own emancipation from the dictates of irrational or unjust habits, customs, precedents, coercion, or bureaucratic systemization ... it also has the aim of emancipation of participants in the action from the dictates or compulsions of tradition, precedent, habit, coercion or self-deception.[196]

In another article Wilfred Carr demanded political commitment by professional educators, providing, of course, that the commitment is to what he terms 'emancipatory educational ideas and values' and the solution of 'problems of irrationality and injustice'.[197] Carr is too coy to spell out which countries so far have had the benefit of this particular type of emancipation, but we can be fairly confident that Britain is not among them, either before or after the 1997 general election, although it is no doubt still a paradigm case of irrationality and injustice, despite Carr's best efforts. Carr is clear, however, about the nature of the critical educational inquiry he advocates. It holds that 'rationality is always relative to time and place' and that there is no 'distinction between the "knowing subject" and an "objective"

---

196 Carr, W. and Kemmis, S. (1993). 'Action Research in Education' in M. Hammersley. *Controversies in Classroom Research*, 2nd ed. Philadelphia: Open University Press, pp. 235; 239; 242
197 Carr, W. (1995). *For Education: Towards Critical Educational Inquiry.* Milton Keynes: Open University Press, pp. 128; 126.

world to be known' and 'no corpus of "objective" knowledge that stands outside the historical context which endows it with meaning and significance'. In the time of Pythagoras it may have appeared that the square on the side of the hypotenuse of a right-angled triangle was equal to the sum of the squares on the other two sides but, apparently, that may not be the case in People's China or late-capitalist Denmark, or perhaps for women, gays or blacks, who have different perspectives on these matters. If they jump out of a high-rise building they may rise rather than fall: critical thinkers would not be dogmatic about such matters, however great their certainty about seemingly more elusive ones. Like other 'critical' and 'reflective' neo-Marxists, Wilfred Carr illustrates the paradox of the liar: he tells his students that there are no objective truths, but assures them that what he tells them is objectively true.

Martin Hammersley, editor of the book in which the Carr and Kemmis article appeared, noted in 1996 that 'taught masters and doctoral level courses are an expanding part of the market and often have substantial theory components'.[198] The most pervasive type of theory remained the type expounded by Wilfred Carr. Several educational journals return manuscripts to their authors if there is a failure to refer to the works of the leading 'critical' and 'reflective' thinkers who exercise a real ideological hegemony whilst frequently deploring the grip exerted by the ruling classes and their lackeys on the educational branches of the ideological state apparatus.

The hegemony of New Left thinking often influences educational research carried out by people who are by no means neo-Marxist ideologues. Rod Bramald, Frank Hardman and David Leat of the University of Newcastle investigated changes to or from two supposed dichotomies of 'pupil-centred' and 'teacher-centred' pedagogies among 162 student secondary teachers in their PGCE year. The 'pupil-centred' position was typified by the researchers as being 'developed from a constructivist philosophy of learning, characterised by statements emphasising interactive work, problem solving and pupils' involvement in the planning and assessing of their own work', the second as 'characterised by statements emphasising whole class teaching

---

[198] Hammersley, M. (1996). 'Post Mortem or Post Modern? Some Reflections on British Sociology of Education' in *British Journal of Educational Studies*, 44 (4), p. 399.

with quiet, orderly concentration, written work, and the reporting of grades to parents'.[199] The researchers found that during the PGCE year 'for most groups [by academic subject that is] there was some movement away from the more student-centred end of the scales'. Those subject groups were the History, Mathematics, Modern Foreign Languages and Religious Education groups, but Geography and English students moved towards student-centred positions.

Although they never explicitly stated their own commitments, let alone providing grounds for them, Bramald and his colleagues seemed distressed by their main finding, although cheered by the changes displayed by the Geography and English students. They claimed that students who 'had moved in support of a traditional approach, when questioned about their changes, tended to focus on "class management" issues which seemed to suggest that they were reflecting at what McIntyre (1992) terms the technical level', by implication a rather lowly intellectual condition. On the other hand the researchers assumed that more 'reflection' was displayed by those furthest away from any 'traditional' approach. Students' judgements with which they clearly concurred included:

> English is not so much about knowledge anyway, it's more about processes and being able to write which is some thing you can help them learn themselves. I don't think it's any one experience that I've had, it's just generally you can't tell people what a book or a poem is about, you can't tell them that's how you use a comma, you just have to help them to do it themselves. It's a more gradual change ... You can't teach people about something, you've just got to give them the methods of doing it themselves ... (Imogen, an English student)

> I think that in the beginning I really wanted to know how to teach my subject and then I realised there wasn't an awful lot to teach ... There is a lot to be learned about how pupils learn, the actual cognitive phases and learning skills. (Fiona, a Geography student)[200]

---

199 Bramald, R., Hardman, F. and Leat, D. (1995). 'Initial Teacher Trainees and Their Views of Teaching and Learning' in *Teaching and Teacher Education* 11 (1), pp. 24–5.
200 Bramald *et al.*, 1995, p. 29.

The researchers commented:

> It is almost certainly true that the two curriculum tutors with the strongest leanings towards experiential learning and reflective practice run the English course (jointly) and the Geography course (singly). In these two courses reflective practice is openly espoused and operated ... Reflection is a word commonly used in these curriculum sessions.[201]

In a report presented to OFSTED in 1998 James Tooley, University of Newcastle, and Doug Darby, University of Manchester, found that in an analysis of four journals taken as representative of British educational research publications, although 'a minority of articles showed a detached, non-partisan approach to the subject studied', the majority were unsatisfactory. Out of a sub-sample of 41 articles appearing between 1994 and 1996 Tooley and Darby found the following percentages as not satisfying 'good practice' in research: *British Educational Research Journal* 73 per cent, *British Journal of Sociology of Education* 70 per cent, *British Journal of Educational Studies* 64 per cent and *Oxford Review of Education* 44 per cent, the overall average being 63 per cent unsatisfactory.[202] No wonder that David Hargreaves dismissed what he called

> frankly second-rate educational research which does not make a serious contribution to fundamental theory or knowledge; which is irrelevant to practice; which is unco-ordinated with any preceding or follow-up research; and which clutters up academic journals that virtually nobody reads.[203]

However, just as the answer to bad theory is good theory, not no theory, so the answer to bad research is better research. But I do not pretend that it will be easy to break the grip of an ideological control which was scarcely weakened, if at all, by over a decade and a half of allegedly intrusive Conservative governments.

---

201 Bramald *et al.*, 1995, 30.
202 Tooley with Darby, 1998, pp. 7; 76.
203 Hargreaves, D. (1996). *Teaching as a Research-based Profession: Possibilities and Prospects.* The Teacher Training Agency Annual Lecture, 1996, p. 7.

7 | Which way ahead?

Most organisations concerned with the promotion of liberal ideas found themselves during the years of the Thatcher and Major governments confronted with dilemmas in educational policy. It was easy enough to identify what was not wanted, but very difficult to depict just what should be sought. In educational policy as a whole, desire to free up the system from centralist bureaucratic controls conflicted with determination to use central power to reduce abuses, raise standards and at last give some real meaning to slogans of educational opportunity, which had become entirely hollow when applied to many state schools long exposed to New Left ideas and practices. In teacher education some support was given to 'bottom-up' reforms, especially through a wider range of modes of entry into teaching, but their effects were bound to be slow, so that far more energy was put into 'top-down' reforms, aiming at ensuring that new entrants into teaching possessed the basic knowledge to teach those parts of the new National Curriculum for which they were responsible and were competent in classroom organisation and management. Now that other hands are on the central educational controls, even though in education 'New Labour' has perhaps more in common with the former 'New Right' than with the earlier 'New Left', liberal thinkers must review the situation once more.

The case for more prescription

There can be no doubt that at school level the National Curriculum, backed by OFSTED, helped to turn the tide, even though most of the battle for educational standards has still to be fought and won, irrespective of under whose banner the struggles are engaged. There is no doubt either that in ITT the National Curriculum, backed by the TTA, has increased competence and efficiency and has made far better use of schools as a positive resource in teacher education than in the past. My uncovering, on very brief investigation, of many unsavoury remnants of indoctrination in ITT will no doubt further convince some that what ITT needs is a still larger dose of the same medicine as before.

Those who think in this way will gain encouragement from Diane Ravitch, one of the most penetrating of American educational critics, who recently suffered a major life-threatening illness. After her recovery, Ravitch compared the way in which medical experts diagnosed and then treated her condition with the way in which educationists might have gone about it:

> The first thing that I noticed was the disappearance of the certainty that the physicians had shared. Instead, my new specialists began to argue over whether anything was actually wrong with me. A few thought that I had a problem, but others scoffed and said that such an analysis was tantamount to 'blaming the victim'. Some challenged the concept of 'illness', claiming it was a social construction, utterly lacking in objective reality. Others rejected the evidence of the tests used to diagnose my ailment: a few said the tests were meaningless for anyone under any circumstances. One of the noisier researchers maintained that any effort to focus attention on my individual situation merely diverted attention from gross social injustices; a just social order, he claimed, could not come into existence until anecdotal cases like mine were not eligible for attention and resources.
>
> Among the raucous crowd of education experts, there was no agreement, no common set of standards for diagnosing my problem. They could not agree on what was wrong with me, perhaps because they did not agree on standards for good health ... A few researchers continued to insist that something was wrong with me; one even pulled out the results of my CAT-scan and sonogram. But the rest ridiculed the tests, pointing that they represented only a snap-shot of my actual condition and were therefore completely unreliable, as compared to longitudinal data.

Ravitch concluded with the reflection

> In our society, we rightly insist upon valid medical research; after all, lives are at risk. Now that I am on the mend, I wonder: Why don't we insist with equal vehemence on well-tested, validated education research? Lives are at risk here, too.[204]

---

204 Ravitch, D. (1998). 'What if Research Really Mattered?' in *Education Week*, 18 (16), pp. 33–4.

One is reminded of Margaret Thatcher's thought that it would be an easy matter to obtain agreement about 'a basic syllabus for English, Mathematics and Science with simple tests to show what pupils knew', since 'It always seemed to me that a small committee of good teachers ought to be able to pool their experience and write down a list of topics and sources to be covered without too much difficulty'.[205]

The case for more freedom

Witty and in many ways wise as Diane Ravitch may be in her castigation of educationists to fail to act as physicians do, she fails to understand the fundamental significance of educational contestability. Although there are many important controversies within medicine at many levels, it is not an essentially contestable subject in the same way in which education is, together, for that matter, with politics. There is essential agreement about what it means to be a healthy person, but not about what it means to be a well-educated person.

Margaret Thatcher's belief that it would be very easy to construct a basic syllabus that would satisfy all, except a small number of identifiably depraved or subversive cranks, is very reminiscent of the search during the nineteenth century for a simple form of 'common Christianity' which all board schools could use without risk of religious controversy. That proved a most elusive quest. For the Thatcher and Major governments, too, as James Tooley has noted, 'competing visions' and the 'knowledge problem' soon arose in almost every subject advisory committee concerned with the National Curriculum.[206] There is always an element of paradox in arguments for uniformity: if all were agreed on what is needed, there would be no need to enforce it. Enforcement only moves on to the agenda when some people find that others decline to accept what they are confident is in their best interests or that of the public. In Tooley's words

> Now, if everyone agreed on the common core curriculum, there would be no need to impose it on schools. So, clearly, it must be

---

205 Thatcher, 1993, p. 593.
206 Tooley, J. (1996). *Education Without The State.* London: Institute of Economic Affairs, pp. 68–79.

controversial, or not what individuals or communities would themselves seek from schooling.[207]

The more culturally diverse a society, the more severe the clash of competing visions. The Canadian educationist Mark Holmes has drawn attention to the inability of what he terms 'low doctrine' public school systems, designed to be minimally disturbing to all beliefs, to foster any coherent set of positive values. This is a serious weakness in contemporary British education. Yet any attempts to enforce non-consensual values on all children must result in resentment and conflict. The 'problem of knowledge' arises even in the most monocultural modern society: the amount of significant knowledge relevant to children and potentially accessible by them is too vast to be enshrined in any compulsory curriculum, so that disputes necessarily arise about what should be included. Whether the curriculum as a whole is under consideration or the content of a single subject, there are massive difficulties in balancing the virtues of breadth, with its risk of superficiality, and depth, with its risk of narrowness or premature specialisation. The controversies in the United States following the publication of E. D. Hirsch Jr's *Cultural Literacy: What Every American Needs To Know* illustrate the difficulties in obtaining agreement among the like-minded, let alone those of different cultural and ideological persuasions.[208]

In end-of-the-millennium Britain, let alone across any greater extent of time and space, some thoughtful people hold that to be well-educated requires some knowledge of at least one classical language, some require instead two or at least one modern language, whereas others hold that knowledge of foreign languages to be, although highly desirable, by no means essential. Some require that each student should experience significant exposure to geometry, algebra and advanced mathematical ideas, but others would be content if all were at least initiated into accurate simple computations. Some call for 'basic' knowledge of the economy, population and landscape of the main regions of the world, perhaps augmented by much more detailed knowledge of one's own country, but others would

---

207 Tooley, 1996, p. 69.
208 Hirsch, E. D., Jr. (1987). *Cultural Literacy: What Every American Needs to Know*. Boston: Houghton Mifflin.

make geography and economics, perhaps history as well, merely optional studies early on in schooling. Some exhort that schools should supply knowledge of contraception, methods of contracting AIDS, the dangers of smoking or eating beef, 'defensive' road skills, and many other 'practical' skills, but others consider most of these will be picked up outside school, or for other reasons are not essential components of a compulsory curriculum. Some think that the moral formation of children requires that they be brought up in religious belief. Others hold that even to teach children about religion is infringing secular liberty. Some wish to foster the 'lowly heart, which bears the humbler part', but many more in 1999 seek at all costs to keep children's self-esteem very high. And so on.

The National Curriculum for ITT is a good example of its kind, but a good example of something not needed. There is a good case for an exemplary or illustrative National Curriculum and many HEIs would no doubt adopt it; many schools would prefer to appoint teachers who had successfully followed it, since it is unlikely that curriculum committees, however divided, would recommend requirements which were widely unacceptable to the most concerned parties. Yet there is very little to be said in favour of a prescriptive National Curriculum. Far better that providers of ITT should be able to offer independent wares. It is reasonable to require of all institutions which seek public funding for ITT, through vouchers or any other means, that they make publicly available the principles on which their courses are based, their structure and modes of evaluation, but in an open competitive system school authorities should be able to check for themselves whether or not applicants possess the knowledge and skills required in the particular employment. Intending teachers, too, should be credited with the sense to find out what range of courses is on offer and to choose wisely.

Each of the five clusters of educational ideas identified earlier is still capable of establishing schools and related ITT of a highly defensible character. The radical-reconstructionist tradition is by no means discredited or exhausted because so many follies have been carried out in recent years by the New Left. Logically, a healthy radical spirit should not wish to be allied, let alone subservient, to state organs, any more than to be paralysed by Althusserian gloom. The Left, like the Right, has libertarian springs from which it can derive new inspiration. The child-centred tradition, if serious about the unique needs of each child and the implications of individuality, is a natural ally, not of corporate central control, but of education as a market in which many different choices may be made. Transcendentalists, perhaps with some exceptions within British Islam, have for several generations in this country accepted religious diversity and should be among the last people to support state-imposed educational uniformity. Some able liberal educators, fearful of the crude instrumentalism often expressed by pupils, parents and employers, have favoured state direction, at least if and when people of their own way of thinking influence governments One thinks of T. H. Green, Arthur Acland, Robert Burdon Haldane, Henry Jones, Michael Sadler and Robert Morant, followed in the next generation by R. H. Tawney, Fred Clarke and A. D. Lindsay. Yet, although the Althusserian thesis was ludicrously exaggerated, liberal educators should fear the temptation for governments, once possessed of sufficient power, to politicise curricula and to place short-term objectives before longer-term aims. Liberal educators should rely upon persuasion, not compulsion, in ITT as in education as a whole.

By a peculiar conjunction of circumstances, with reaction against New Left ideology a significant factor, many adherents of instrumental education in Britain, including some on the political Right, became active supporters of a tightly-knit National Curriculum and it was, of course, a Conservative government which introduced it. This is to some extent fortuitous: in Australia during the 1980s it was the Labor Party (ALP) which most strongly supported a National Curriculum, with the teacher unions in the vanguard of advocacy; in New Zealand the National Party, the equivalent of the British Conservatives, introduced a National Curriculum with a standards system similar to that in England and Wales, but the main centre of opposition has been the Education Forum of the New Zealand Round Table, consisting mainly of market-oriented employers and heads of independent schools. It might appear to be at best inconsistent and at worst rather despicable politicking were the Conservative Party to reject in opposition the National Curriculum it introduced in government, but in the long run it must be in its own political interests, as well as the best instrumentalist strategy for Britain, if choice were given more scope and the National Curriculum changed into an optional model to which a wide range of alternative ways of organising schools and teacher education is not only permitted but encouraged.

The limits of contestability

It is important to distinguish between the contestable and the arbitrary in education. I have already urged that in an open and democratic society there can justifiably be considerable diversity of opinion as to what constitutes successful educational practice, that this justifiable diversity is a fundamental reason why there should be a wide range of choice in education and why intending teachers should have adequate exposure to the competing cases for different educational priorities. This exposure is, I fully concede, difficult to achieve in SCITT, although to be sure many education departments in HEIs dismally fail to present alternative views of the educational good in a fair way to their trainee teachers. However, these arguments for choice and diversity in teacher education, as in education as a whole, do not imply that there is no objective knowledge which all those engaged in educational contestation ought to acknowledge. As Paul Hirst put the point:

> Professional practice is no such thing unless it is based on a body of knowledge and generalisation which has public rational defence way beyond anything that individuals can personally synthesise and test ... teachers should not be trained to see themselves as primarily developing a personal professional stance. Rather they should see themselves as part of a professional group working towards an ever greater consensus about practice. Students are then to be trained by initiation into the most defensible practices to date and into the search for the further development of these.[209]

Hirst's position was challenged by Donald McIntyre who holds that 'in the light of the research, scholarship and argument of the last twenty years it has become virtually impossible to sustain a case that teacher education can or should be a matter of induction into recommended practices "based on a body of knowledge and generalisation which has public rational defence"'.[210] McIntyre agreed with the claim of the American

---

209 Hirst, P. (1990). 'Internship: A View from Outside' in P. Benton. *The Oxford Internship Scheme: Integration and Partnership in Initial Teacher Education*. London: Calouste Gulbenkian Foundation, p. 153.
210 McIntyre, D. (1995). 'Initial Teacher Education as Practical Theorising: A Response to Paul Hirst' in *British Journal of Educational Studies*, XXXXIII (4), p. 373.

psychologist Cronbach that 'research seeking generalizable knowledge about teaching was futile because of the multiplicity of interacting factors and the constantly changing nature of social realities'.[211] If McIntyre is right and there are no practices into which beginning teachers should be inducted, then there is no case at all for ITT, whether based in schools or HEIs. But McIntyre and Cronbach are wrong, and there is such a case.

What are the limits that may, indeed ought, to be placed on educational contestability? The most important justification for exclusion from contestation is refusal to permit contestation. The 'paradox of freedom' is that the liberty of some to impose their will on others must be constrained in the interests of the liberty of all. Precisely how far to tolerate the politically or educationally intolerant is, of course, a permanent problem, difficult to resolve. Governments are also morally entitled to ensure that schools and teacher educators do not incite their students to break the law or infringe the rights of others, but that restraint is incumbent on all associations in civil society. Secondary possible grounds for exclusion from contestability include refusal, or failure, to offer criteria of educational success and evidence by which it can be determined whether or not these are being met.

Are there any grounds on which some modes of teacher education might justifiably be restricted? A critical case in transcendental education today relates to Islam. Demands made by Muslims include single sex schools after the age of puberty, traditionally appropriate dress for each sex, science teaching in accord with the Koran, and prohibition of representational art, especially of the human figure, and many western forms of music. The full programme of Islam requires rote learning by early adolescence of the whole Koran and mastery of the classical Arabic in which it is written. Quite clearly, teachers for such an Islamic education could not be adequately prepared in standard ITT, however rhetorically powerful its claims to be multicultural. Of course, many Muslims who demand freedom for Islamic ITT in Britain oppose toleration of non-Islamic education in Islamic societies, but exposure of double standards does not provide an adequate basis for public policy. Provided that incitement to reduce the religious and political freedoms of

---

211 McIntyre's reference was to Cronbach, J. (1975). 'Beyond the Two Disciplines of Scientific Psychology' in *American Psychologist*, 30 (2), pp. 116–127.

other groups is forbidden, together with infliction of illegal punishments, the balance lies in favour of permitting Islamic ITT on the same terms as Christian and Jewish education.

Are there any grounds on which child-centred or reconstructionist teacher education might justifiably be restricted? There are some reconstructionists who might, if they came to power, put an end to contestation and impose on all their own beliefs but, although I deplore their negative influence, I doubt they can succeed in subverting the social and political order. They will be found, not on barricades, but at international conferences of educators. The paradox of freedom does not in this case lead us to consider restrictions on the would-be restrictors.

I am not suggesting that England and Wales should return to the situation before the Conservative reforms in ITT in which the award of an academic qualification by a college or university constituted in itself a licence to teach, limited only by the fragile requirements of a probationary teaching year. It may well be that some BEd or PGCE awards do not deserve to be recognised for QTS. Yet there are many ways to be a good teacher even in a single and very specific area and providers of ITT, SCITT groups and HEIs alike, should be able to put forward ITT structures which may differ significantly in their balance from that of the National Curriculum for ITT of the moment. There is no particular amount of time to be spent in schools as against in HEIs, or any particular internal course structure which merits compulsory imposition on all. Under the system I envisage the responsibility would fall on the ITT provider to demonstrate to the TTA that those who completed its courses were capable of carrying out satisfactorily the key duties reasonably to be required of beginning teachers in the given area of teaching. Given the prestige usually attached to exemplary models, it is likely that potential teachers will choose carefully before they enter courses which differ from the standard and that employers of teachers will consider carefully what is being offered other than the standard, but variation from the standard would not in itself necessarily be inferior to it.

The positive role of ITT

During the last twenty years I have been among the most conspicuous of critics of teacher education in Australia. My criticisms led to considerable professional and personal difficulties. When on the Left and an active communist within the NUT in

England, I gained promotions very easily, perhaps undeservedly so, whereas my later criticisms of New Left policies made it hard for me to keep my job at all and precluded any promotion, despite a prolific publication record. Thus, in retirement, I have no cause at all to be 'soft' on teacher education. Yet it would be strange if I had entered teacher education in the first place, or remained within it subsequently, unless I believed it had considerable potential for good. It is thus incumbent on me to add to my attacks on the serious deformations which teacher education has suffered in Britain, Australia and many other liberal democracies a defence of its essential justification.

Several severe critics of ITT, such as Sheila Lawlor, have rightly emphasised the priority of specific content in teaching over general aspects of pedagogy. Gaining adequate knowledge has logical precedence over acquiring ways, even the best possible ones if these can be identified, of communicating that knowledge to others. Inculcation of substantive knowledge is not, of course, the exclusive field of ITT but, if not constantly attended to, other courses will be studied to little purpose. Content knowledge affects not only what teachers teach but how they teach it. Teachers with depth of knowledge are more likely to stress conceptual understanding and to see many connections between different elements of study, whereas non-specialists more often simply teach the content as represented in a prescribed text.[212] There can be no doubt that weaknesses in substantive knowledge provide the greatest single group of shortcomings among teachers, especially primary teachers.

One can thus well understand how angry people like Sheila Lawlor must become when they encounter denials of these basic truths made by leading figures in ITT. Publications issued by UCET frequently challenge the primacy of subject knowledge and allege that the criteria employed by TTA and OFSTED 'over-emphasise the extent of a teacher's personal knowledge at the expense of pedagogic content knowledge'.[213] Anne Edwards

---

[212] See Grossman, P. I., Wilson, S. M. and Shulman, L. E. (1989). 'Teachers of Substance: Subject Matter Knowledge for Teaching' in Reynolds, M. C. (ed). *Knowledge Base for the Beginning Teacher.* New York: Pergamon; McDiarmid, G. W., Ball, D. L. and Anderson, C. W. (1989).'Why Staying One Chapter Ahead Doesn't Really Work: Subject Specific Pedagogy' in Reynolds (ed).

[213] Those words are from Richards *et al.*, 1997, p. 51.

of the University College of St Martin, University of Lancaster, has elaborated the argument against the primacy of subject knowledge. She criticised the 'current emphasis, evident in the U.K. at least, on an input-output view of the transmission of subject knowledge at both the primary and secondary phases of education' and urged that 'the very notion of application of subject matter needs to be questioned in the context of initial teacher training'. She claimed that 'what is applied in classrooms is subject-specific pedagogical knowledge which has enabled teachers to understand how they might translate their conceptual frameworks to meet the learning needs of pupils. These needs are diagnosed by teachers who draw on both their understandings of children's thinking and motivation and a developmentally framed understanding of those key concepts in a subject that constitutes the curriculum'.[214] Edwards recommended a much-favoured radical constructivist solution to problems of learning and teaching: 'a neo-Vygotskian model' which will ensure 'a seamless pedagogically driven partnership in which role overlap is a central feature'. Translated into clearer terms, Edwards' claim is that people who do not know much about mathematics, science, language structures, or whatever may be the content to be learned, but who have been on courses about neo-Vygotskian constructivism, are more likely to be effective teachers than people with considerable substantive knowledge of the relevant subject matter, but who have not been initiated into constructivist pedagogies. Were this the case, there would be no such thing as 'shortage' subjects, since all who were initiated into constructivism would soon to be able to teach anything. Anne Edwards' line is congenial to teacher unions, since it implies that every teacher, whether a driving instructor, archaeologist, soccer coach, reception class teacher, or physicist, is essentially a teacher like unto other teachers.

However, rejection of inflated claims for pedagogical knowledge, such as those of Anne Edwards, does not entail that even successful study of a subject is a sufficient as well as a necessary condition for teaching it successfully. This is true even of specialist subject teaching in secondary schools. There are serious problems of poor fit between graduate courses in the main substantive disciplines taught in schools and the requirements

---

214 Edwards, A. (1995). 'Teacher Education: Partnerships in Pedagogy?' in *Teaching and Teacher Education*, 11 (6), p. 598.

posed by school syllabuses. Some of these problems have been highlighted by the National Curriculum. Many university arts and humanities departments do not even claim to offer broad-based degree courses, but instead choose topics largely on the basis of the research interests of academic staff. With university promotion and scholarly esteem dependent mainly on research publications in depth, there is an understandable reluctance among lecturers to teach broad courses unless they are compelled to do so. Although courses focused on lecturers' research interests often have high intrinsic value and provide considerable intellectual stimulation, they may not be optimal preparation for secondary school teaching of, say, history or English.

Furthermore, science degree courses naturally concentrate almost exclusively on the concerns of a specific discipline, whereas the secondary science teacher typically has to teach integrated or interdisciplinary courses in the first three years of secondary schools before teaching specialised physics, chemistry or biology courses in senior classes. Many graduate physicists lack basic information and concepts needed to teach the biology components of junior secondary science in the National Curriculum, and biology graduates are often very deficient in physics. This remains a problem even if there are fewer interdisciplinary or integrated courses, since in smaller schools most science teachers are required to teach a minor subject together with the main one. There are also good grounds for supposing that some general understanding of the nature and history of science is, apart from its intrinsic value, likely to be helpful to intending science teachers, but a 1994 study concluded that 'teachers' lack of knowledge about the nature of science emerged strongly in the study' and 'the lack of reflection was most apparent in the neglect of the cultural, moral and philosophical aspects of science'.[215] However, instead of ITT tackling this weakness, together with serious deficiencies in specific content of various sciences, with all possible energy, what has often happened is that, as Michael Matthews has put it, 'under the influence of child-centred

---

215 Lakin, S. and Wellington, J. (1994). 'Who will Teach "the Nature of Science"? Teachers' Views of Science and their Implications for Science Education' in *International Journal of Science Education*, 16 (2), p. 186 [cited in Matthews, M. (1995). *Challenging NZ Science Education*. Palmerston North: Dunmore Press, p. 203]. My discussion of constructivism is indebted to Matthews' analysis.

constructivism, more and more time is taken up learning about "children's science"'. The solution to such weaknesses is not for governments to try to force universities to follow, or anticipate, the demands of secondary school syllabuses, but there is certainly a great need for responsible academics, school teachers and administrators to become clear themselves about the types of poor fit which currently abound and to engage in ongoing discussions about what constitute sufficient conditions for effective teaching and successful learning in the various subjects of the school curriculum.

Problems in teachers' knowledge bases are generally most serious in early childhood and primary education, as the Exeter research of Bennett and Carre showed. Arguments in favour of integrated or thematic teaching in the education of young children are often undermined because teachers lack the knowledge to make appropriate connections. The more integrated or interdisciplinary the curriculum, the greater the need to understand links between different aspects of a subject and relationships between different sorts of knowledge. It is in this sense that it can be seriously claimed that the preparation of teachers of young children is an intellectually demanding undertaking. In practice, however, cognitive demands have been comparatively low, as has been clearly understood by many who have applied to enter early childhood rather than other kinds of teaching. Although his claim excited union antagonism, Dennis O'Keeffe was only following the personal beliefs of many practitioners when he argued that 'what you want to be a teacher of the very young is to be a highly literate, highly numerate person who likes children and is good at teaching them, and good at controlling them', irrespective of any possible shortcomings in other types of academic knowledge.[216] In his review of the Exeter study Jim Campbell observed that 'the image of the Early Years teacher' it conveyed was of 'women, mathematically and scientifically inadequate though reasonably competent in language'.[217]

Because teachers of young children have very limited knowledge in many areas of their teaching, they are often even more vulnerable than secondary teachers to ideological bandwagons. Provided the message is wrapped up in warm and empathetic

---

216 O'Keeffe, 1990, p. 14
217 Campbell, R. J. (1994). Review of *Learning to Teach* in *Teaching and Teacher Education*, 10 (2), p. 255.

child-centred language, and the deliverer seems both authoritative and politically correct, many are easily persuaded of the virtue of innovations, as with open plan classrooms and whole-book reading. This mindset cannot easily be changed, but more specialised knowledge is likely to reduce vulnerability to ideological quackery, as well as give early childhood teachers a more realistic range within which to achieve a high level of competence.

The National Curriculum for ITT has already made far more professional demands on teachers of young children than they had faced before, a shift in the opposite direction indicated by the almost simultaneous Conservative attempt to recruit 'Mum's Army' to teach these same young children. If stronger subject knowledge is still required from early childhood and primary teachers, this is more likely to result from well-organised and demanding ITT courses, despite past failures to provide these consistently, than from individual efforts to remedy weaknesses in the midst of classroom work.

However, the obdurate fact is that it is extremely difficult for generalist teachers of young children to achieve a high level of competence in every major subject in the curriculum, let alone in all other desirable non-core subjects. An important step towards higher standards in early childhood and primary education would be to abandon the ideal of one teacher who seeks to integrate the entire curriculum and, instead, to introduce a simple but powerful division of labour. Many parents are keen to spend good money on giving their young children a really proficient piano, violin, cricket, tennis or dance and drama teacher, yet our primary schools usually fail to provide anything near the level of expertise which could be made available at no extra cost to the public purse, if the glorification of the all-purpose facilitator were jettisoned. Sufficient improvements needed in the core subjects are unlikely to be achieved unless teachers are more knowledgable. But it is extremely difficult for them to become sufficiently knowledgable across the full range of the curriculum.

The situation in ITT is far from uniformly bleak and those, like Sheila Lawlor, who are rightly concerned about cavalier attitudes to substantive knowledge expressed by some leading figures in ITT, can readily find work in the field that should please them more. There does not seem much of a gap between Lawlor's essential concerns and those of the influential American educationist L. E. Shulman, whose conclusions were summarised by David McNamara of the University of Hull School of Education as follows:

> If the aim of teaching is to enhance children's understanding, then teachers themselves must have a flexible and sophisticated understanding of subject matter knowledge in order to achieve this purpose in the classroom.
>
> At the heart of teaching is the notion of forms of representation and to a significant degree teaching entails knowing about and understanding ways of representing and formulating subject matter knowledge so that it can be understood by children. This in turn requires teachers to have a sophisticated understanding of a subject and its interaction with other subjects.
>
> Teachers' subject matter knowledge influences the way in which they teach and teachers who know more about a subject will be more interesting and adventurous in the ways in which they teach and more effective. Teachers with only a limited knowledge of a subject may avoid teaching difficult or complex aspects of it and teach in a didactic manner which avoids pupil participation and questioning and fails to draw upon children's experience.
>
> Knowledge of subject content is necessary to enable the teacher to evaluate text books, computer software and other teaching aids and mediums of instruction.
>
> During their own education student teachers will have acquired knowledge of subjects in both school and during their higher education courses. They may therefore have developed attitudes towards the way in which a subject is studied and misunderstandings which need rectifying if they are to teach their subject successfully in school.[218]

To be sure, the first qualification to be a teacher is to possess adequate knowledge of what is to be taught. A good mathematics teacher must be at least a competent mathematician, and so on. At the same time a good maths teacher, as distinct from a good instructor in how to calculate compound interest,

---

218 McNamara, D. (1991). 'Subject Knowledge and its Application: Problems and Possibilities for Teacher Educators' in *Journal of Education for Teaching*, 17 (2), p. 115. A good short account of Shulman's ideas is his 1986 'Those Who Understand: Knowledge Growth in Teaching' in *Educational Researcher*, 15 (2), pp. 4–14.

needs to know what relationships exist between different mathematical ideas and processes, and also how mathematical understanding can best be fostered among students. At a more general level, the good mathematics teacher will be interested in how understanding of mathematics relates to other kinds of understanding: to scientific understanding, say, and even to the development of the human mind as a whole. There is no automatic transformation of substantive scholarship into curriculum content, let alone self-generated linking of different sorts of knowledge. It is difficult even for a first-rate scholar to shape knowledge in ways in which children are best able to understand it and make it their own. To be a capable historian of whatever period or subject does not in itself enable one to choose curriculum content in the best way or to develop the best ways in which pupils may tackle it. To be an excellent mathematician does not in itself qualify one on how to introduce pupils to the structures and language of elementary mathematics.

Just as the justification by Shulman and McNamara of the potential, if not always the actual, value of ITT in relating substantive knowledge to the minds of children should appeal to liberal conservatives, so should the justifications of the place of general educational ideas in ITT offered by educational thinkers such as Paul Hirst. Michael Oakeshott, who has been very influential with many conservative thinkers about education, argued that

> practical knowledge can neither be taught nor learned, but only imparted and acquired. It exists only in practice, and the only way to acquire it is by apprenticeship to a master – not because the master can teach it (he cannot), but because it can be acquired only by continuous contact with one who is perpetually practising it.[219]

In respect of activities of a non-contestable character this is broadly right. The practical knowledge required to be a good blacksmith, for example, is mainly acquired by continuous contact with a master smith, although even in that case some scientific knowledge beyond that acquirable through observation and imitation of exemplary practice will help a good smith to be a better one. In the first phase of the industrial revolution in Britain many major inventions were made by men who had

---

219 Fuller, T. (ed) (1989). *The Voice of Liberal Learning : Michael Oakeshott on Education.* New Haven: Yale University Press, p. 11.

very little scientific knowledge, such as Samuel Crompton and James Hargreaves, but it is a commonplace of economic history that this has not recurred in later phases of industrial development, such as those in chemicals and electronics. Teaching is a paradigm case of an activity in which observation and imitation of masters of the art is insufficient to achieve optimum effectiveness or adequate understanding.

Paul Hirst was surely right when he expressed doubts whether 'practical "common sense"', based on the process of trial and error, can be relied upon to find the best ways to teach children or what to teach them.[220] He argued that 'the "common sense" of teachers as developed in practice that never calls basic beliefs into question' is 'riddled with unexamined premises which are not to be trusted'.[221] This is to reject, not the importance of practice, but uncritical acceptance of traditional lore. We should recognise with Popper that the great corpus of knowledge now available to us was built up only because sanctified beliefs of tribal and other closed societies were challenged, and that modern totalitarian regimes threatened knowledge by new forms of closure. Our task is to combine respect for established practices and ideas with a willingness to re-examine and if necessary challenge them. Frequent gross misuse of terms such as 'critical' and 'reflective' is no warrant for any failure on our part to ensure that teachers begin their professional lives aware of the basic ideas which underlie current practices and of the possible grounds on which we might seek to revise some of them or even abandon them.

Much criticism of educational disciplines as irrelevant to the practical problems of classrooms is fundamentally misconceived. To be knowledgable about changing practices in the control of children does not in itself, of course, make one an expert on how to deal with children who are bullies, vandals or thieves, or their victims. To be knowledgable about relationships between social status and educational achievement does not, in itself, enable one to determine whether curricula or teaching methods should be as similar, or dissimilar, as possible for all groups. To understand differences between needs and wants does not

---

220 Hirst, 1993, p. 85.
221 Hirst, P. H. (1990). 'The Theory–Practice Relationship in Teacher Training' in M. Booth, J. Furlong and M. Wilkin (eds). *Partnership in Initial Teacher Training*. London: Cassell, p. 77.

in itself enable one to decide whether what a particular child wants constitutes an educational need, let alone how to satisfy it should it be held to be so. These wider understandings are not only insufficient to ensure efficient teaching, but it may even be that they are not always necessary in the short run, since some instructional tasks can be undertaken successfully without any need for thought about any aims of education. Yet it is hard to believe that teachers will not benefit from such knowledge and understanding.

Conclusion

The New Left ascendancy established during the 1960s led to the proliferation of bad educational ideas and theories in ITT. Conservative policies were a justifiable response to a disgraceful situation which the formal machinery of academic controls scarcely touched. The 'bottom-up' reforms opened up new routes into teaching and in themselves constituted a significant challenge to HEIs to improve their own courses. This is very true of SCITT, even though school-based ITT is likely to remain a minor path into teaching, not the main road. The activities of OFSTED and the TTA have helped to bring about substantial improvements in the quality of relationships between schools and HEIs, especially in the organisation of teaching practice, although it would be wrong to imagine that there, or elsewhere in ITT, a formula has been discovered which all should be compelled to adopt. The new system of competencies, now standards, has helped to eliminate a lot of inefficiency and slackness in ITT, as many teacher educators acknowledge. Indeed, despite widespread resentment towards what they regard as undue harshness in the inspectorial system, many teacher educators claim that they had already initiated many of the changes which the TTA has made obligatory. Yet a compulsory curriculum implies that there is a model system of ITT which all should follow, and this is not the case. Whatever may have been the justification for introducing the harsh medicine of compulsion, the case for converting a National Curriculum into an exemplary instead of a prescriptive model is very powerful.

That many current courses concerning race and gender, and much besides, are still biased and indoctrinative may appear to strengthen the case for even more severe reductions in the amount of time devoted in ITT to general educational ideas. In many ways it is easier for ideological poison to be administered in 'anti-sexism' and 'anti-racism' courses now that there are few other ways in which ITT students meet with educational theory of any sort. New Left ideology, with all the 'revolutionary defeatism' and negativity discussed above, is still powerful in ITT after all the Conservative reforms have run their course. One reason for its survival may have been the willingness of some of the New Right to reject not only bad theory but all theory if possible. This stance, easily labelled as anti-intellectual, alienated many educators who were by no means sympathetic to neo-Marxism or the Left in general, weakened the overall thrust of the Conservative reforms, and unnecessarily isolated many of those who advocated them. It is now time for reconsideration. The best answer to bad theory is good theory, not no theory. Moreover, Conservatives should ponder on their failure to win the support of some of the teacher educators I interviewed in 1997. They were enthusiastic about the overall effects of Conservative policies in ITT on the balance of their own pre-service courses and on their relationships with schools which are now their senior partners in teaching practice. Nevertheless, they felt that there was an unfair ideological animus against ITT in any shape among some Conservative ministers and New Right authors.

Policies in the field of ITT should not be based on the assumption that every teacher educator is incompetent, or hardened against the idea that education is essentially contestable, or opposed to all serious attempts to reduce slackness and to raise educational standards. Ways can be found and must be found to enlist more support within ITT, both in HEIs and the schools, for the reclamation of British education from the sad condition to which it was reduced by the New Left. Important first steps towards educational recovery were taken by the Thatcher and Major governments and some of these have been continued under the aegis of Mr Blair and Mr Blunkett. Much remains to be done, and I do not suggest that it is very much easier in 1999 than in 1979 to achieve the best balance between 'bottom-up' policies of opening up ITT to much greater choice and variety of approach and 'top-down' policies focused on central specification and enforcement of higher levels of teacher competency. As I have made clear, my own emphasis is on opening up ITT to new providers, including the schools themselves, but I do not deny the strength of the case for greater rigour, provided that we can resolve the ancient problem of *quis custodiet ipsos custodes?*: who will guard the guards themselves?

Appendix A: Some Reading Lists

The following three reading lists are representative of what I found to be generally offered in 1997 in ITT courses which purported to be countering sexism or racism. Some of the publications recommended are well worth reading, but I find it hard to believe that any responsible educator would regard any of these lists as fair coverage of informed and legitimate contributions to those issues. Where publication details are not given in full, it is because they were not supplied in the original reading lists.

University of Manchester

PGCE: reading list for 'Race, culture and education' section of its Living and Learning in a Plural Britain part 1

Bourne, J. et al. (1994). *Outcast England – How Schools Exclude Black Children*. Institute of Race Relations.
DES (1985). *Education for All* (The Swann Report). HMSO.
Gaine, C. (1987). *No Problem Here;* (1997). *Still No Problem Here*. Trentham Books.
Hulme, E. (1989). *Education and Cultural Diversity*. Longman.
Klein, G. (1993). *Education towards Race Equality*. Cassell.
MacDonald, I. (1989). *Murder in the Playground – the Report of the MacDonald Inquiry into Racism and Racial Violence in Manchester Schools*. Longsight Press.
Mohood, T. et al. *Ethnic Minorities in Britain*. Policy Studies Institute.
Owen, D. (1995). *Ethnic Minorities in Britain*. Warwick: Centre for Ethnic Relations.
Pumphrey, P. D and Verma, G. K. (eds) (1993–4). *Cultural Diversity and the Curriculum*. 4 vols. Lewes: Falmer Press.
Troyna, B. (1993). *Racism and Education – Research Perspectives*. Open University.

Verma, G. K. (ed). *Education for All – A Landmark in Pluralism*. Lewes: Falmer Press.

Verma, G. K., Sec. F. and Skinner, G. D. (1992). *The Ethnic Crucible – Harmony and Hostility in Multiethnic Schools*. Falmer Press.

Visram, R. (1986). *Ayahs, Lascars and Princes*. Pluto Press.

Manchester Metropolitan University
Professional Issues Resources Book
Recommended Readings on Gender and Race

Arnot, M. and Wiener, G. (1987). *Gender and the Politics of Schooling*. Open University Press.

Askew, S. and Ross, C. (1988). *Boys Don't Cry: Boys and Sexism in Education*. Open University Press.

Deem, R. (1984). *Co-education Reconsidered*. Open University Press.

Delamont, S. (1990). *Sex Roles and the School*. Routledge.

Donnellan, C. (1995). *Disabilities and Equality*. Independence, (all three).
Our Aging Generation
Our Sexist World

Gaine, C. (1990). *Still No Problem Here: Teaching about Race and Social Justice*. Trentham.

Leicester, M. (1991). *Equal Opportunities in School*. Longman.

Massey, I. (1991). *More Than Skin Deep: Developments in Anti-racist and Multicultural Education in School*. London: Hodder & Stoughton.

Myers, K. (1987). *Genderwatch: Self-assessment Schedules*. SCDC.

National Union of Teachers. *Towards Equality for Girls and Boys: Guidelines on Countering Sexism in Schools*.

Rudduck, J. (1994). *Developing a Gender Policy in Secondary Schools*. Open University Press.

Runnymede Trust. *Equality Assurance: A Handbook for Action in Schools*. Trentham.

Sewell, T. (1997). *Black Masculinities and Schooling*. Trentham.

Spender, D. (1980). *Man Made Language*. Routledge.

Stanworth, M. (1981). *Gender and Schooling*. Hutchinson.

The Girls and Occupational Choice Project. Hidden Messages: An Equal Opportunities Teaching Pack. Oxford: Blackwell, 1987.

Thompson, S. (1986). *Alright for Some – The Problem of Sexism.* Hutchinson.
Verma, G. et al. (1994). *The Ethnic Crucible: Harmony and Hostility in Multi-ethnic Schools.* Lewes: Falmer.
Walkerdine, V. (1989). *Counting Girls Out.* Virago.
Weiner, G. (1985). *Just a Bunch of Girls.* Open University Press.
Whyld, J. (1983). *Sexism in the Secondary Curriculum.* Harper and Rowe.

University of Warwick Institute of Education
PGCE Secondary Courses 1997–1998:
Core Programme Study Guide
Equal Opportunities: race

CRE (1992). *Set to Fail.* London: CRE.
DES (1985). *Education for All The Swan Report* (sic). London: HMSO.
Duncan, C. (1989). *Pastoral Care: an Anti-racist Cultural Perspective.* London: Heinemann.
Massey, I. (1992). *More than Skin Deep: Developing Anti-racist Education in Schools.* Stoke: Trentham Books.
Reiss, M. and King, A. (1993). *The Multicultural Dimension of the National Curriculum.* Lewes: Falmer Press.
Richardson, R. et al. (1994). *Equality Assurance in Schools.* Stoke: Trentham Books.
Tomlinson, S. (1990). *Multicultural Education in White Schools.* London: Macmillan.
Troyna, B. (1995). *Racism and Education.* Milton Keynes: Open University Press.
Verma, G. and Pumphrey, P. (1993). *Cultural Diversity and the Curriculum.* London: Taylor and Francis.

Equal Opportunities: gender

Byrne, E. (1991). *Gender in Education.* London: Cassell.
Messor, L. and Sikes, P. (1990). *Gender in Education.* Milton Keynes: Open University Press.
Ruddock, J. (1994). *Developing a Gender Policy in Schools.* Milton Keynes: Open University Press.
Sikes, P. (1997). *Parents as Teachers.* London: Cassell.
Spender, D. (1978). *Invisible Women.* London: Writers and Readers.
Stanworth, M. (1991). *Gender and Schooling.* London: Kogan Page.

Glossary

ATCDE:	Association of Teachers in Colleges and Departments of Education
ATL:	Association of Teachers and Lecturers
ATO:	Area Training Organisation
AUT:	Association of University Teachers
BEd:	Bachelor of Education
CATE:	Council for the Accreditation of Teacher Education
CNAA:	Council for National Academic Awards
DES:	Department of Education and Science
DfE:	Department for Education
HEI:	Higher Education Institution
HMI:	Her Majesty's Inspectorate
ILEA:	Inner London Education Authority
ITT:	Initial Teacher Training
LEA:	Local Educational Authority
LMS:	Local Management of Schools
MMU:	Manchester Metropolitan University
NATE:	National Association for the Teaching of English
NCC:	National Curriculum Council
NUT:	National Union of Teachers
OFSTED:	The Office for Standards in Education
PGCE:	Post Graduate Certificate of Education
QTS:	Qualified Teacher Status

SCAA:	Schools Curriculum and Assessment Authority
SCITT:	School-Centred Initial Teacher Training
SEAC:	Schools Examinations and Assessment Committee
TTA:	Teacher Training Agency
UCET:	The Universities Council for the Education of Teachers

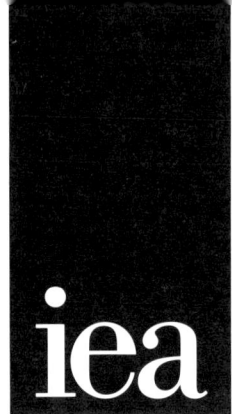

The Global Education Industry

Lessons from Private Education in Developing Countries

James Tooley

Changes in private education now underway in the developing world could have a dramatic impact on the lives of millions worldwide.

Drawing on examples from Argentina, Brazil, Colombia, India, Indonesia, Peru, Romania, Russia, South Africa, Zimbabwe and other countries, Professor Tooley gives a snapshot of private education that may surprise many readers: contrary to expectations, the private education sector is large in the countries studied, it is innovative, and it is not the exclusive domain of the wealthy. The author challenges the conventional wisdom that private education in developing countries fosters greater social and economic inequality; he points out that such education often provides creative social responsibility programmes, subsidised places, and student loan schemes.

James Tooley identifies the factors that impede or facilitate the development of the private education sector in various countries, focusing on the regulatory regimes that may impinge upon private education.

Finally, he considers the ways in which the existence of an innovative private education sector could influence education policy as practised by international agencies and national governments. He concludes with a 'modest proposal' for how for-profit education enterprises could play an important role in promoting equitable development.

The Institute of Economic Affairs
2 Lord North Street, Westminster, London SW1P 3LB
Telephone: 0171 799 3745 Facsimile: 0171 799 2137
E-mail: iea@iea.org.uk Internet: http://www.iea.org.uk

£8.00

ISBN 0-255 36475-X